D0533263

PM-250-AL

ARRELIAS

EYEWITNESS TRAVEL

Left **Tiles, Faro** Right **Roman bridge, Tavira**

LONDON, NEW YORK,
MELBOURNE, MUNICH AND DELHI
www.dk.com

Produced by Blue Island Publishing
Printed and bound in China by Leo Paper
Products Ltd

First published in the UK in 2003 by
Dorling Kindersley Limited
80 Strand, London WC2R 0RL
A Penguin Company

Copyright 2003, 2013 © Dorling Kindersley
Limited, London

13 14 15 16 10 9 8 7 6 5 4 3 2 1

**Reprinted with revisions 2005,
2007, 2009, 2011, 2013**

A CIP catalogue record is available from the
British Library.

ISBN 978 1 4093 7344 5

Within each Top 10 list in this book, no
hierarchy of quality or popularity is implied.
All 10 are, in the editor's opinion, of roughly
equal merit.

Contents

The Algarve's Top 10

Left **Market, Loulé** Right **Café with castle in the background, Alcoutim**

Left **Sagres harbour** Right **Ponta de Piedade, Lagos**

Key to abbreviations
Adm *admission charge payable* **Free** *no admission charge*

THE ALGARVE'S TOP 10

THE ALGARVE'S TOP 10

Highlights of the Algarve

The Moors called their al-Gharb the Sunset Land, and visitors have been waxing lyrical ever since. Blessed with a mild winter climate and a sunny disposition, Portugal's playground province remains one of the most popular year-round holiday destinations in southern Europe. Lively coastal resorts spill over ribbons of golden sand in sharp contrast to the quiet villages of the hinterland, where history and tradition go hand in hand.

Folk dancers

Faro

The biggest city in southern Portugal, Faro is the capital of the Algarve and an important centre of tourism, trade and commerce. Its historic quarter overlooks a pretty marina and the Ria Formosa *(see pp8–11).*

Tavira

Nearly 40 churches endow this elegant riverside town with a romantic and disarmingly timeless air. The Gilão river glides effortlessly through the centre – a Roman bridge connects the two sides of one of the prettiest towns in the Algarve *(see pp12–13).*

Monchique

The Serra da Monchique rises 458 m (1,500 ft), enveloping the hillside town of Monchique and its neighbouring spa centre *(see pp16–17).*

Silves

Once the grandiose capital of the Moorish province of al-Gharb, Silves today is dominated by the ochre ramparts of its huge castle. Lush orange groves blanket the countryside *(see pp14–15).*

Previous pages **Igreja do Carmo, Faro**

Lagos

A young, vibrant and carefree spirit imbues this resort. The nearby beaches, pocked with outcrops of sandstone rock, are spectacular *(see pp20–23)*.

Loulé
Loulé hosts a colourful weekly market and is a thriving centre for local handicrafts. It is also the gateway to the central hinterland and the Caldeirão mountain range *(see pp18–19)*.

Parque Natural da Ria Formosa
One of the most important wetland zones in Europe, the park's expansive lagoon, sand dunes and marshland are a sanctuary for a wealth of wildlife *(see pp24–7)*.

Sagres
The supposed location of Henry the Navigator's lauded school of navigation, Sagres sits on an isolated promontory pounded by the Atlantic. Dramatic views along the coast include the Cabo de São Vicente *(see pp28–9)*.

Albufeira
This top holiday spot is the Algarve's largest resort, boasting some of the most effervescent nightlife in Portugal. Generous beaches flank bustling esplanades brimming with cafés and trendy clubs *(see pp30–31)*.

Vila Real and Castro Marim
These two frontier towns are in earshot of each other but have little in common. Sedate Castro Marim glories in its twin castles. Vila Real de Santo António enjoys a livelier culture *(see pp32–3)*.

Map labels: Alcoutim, Martinlongo, Ribeira da Foupana, Vaqueiros, Ameixial, Guerreiros do Rio, Cachopo, Odeleite, Rocha Da Pena, Azinhal, Salir, Ribeira de Odeleite, Serra de Alcaria do Cume, Querença, Castro Marim, Vila Real de Santo António, São Brás de Alportel, Santa Catarina da Fonte do Bispo, Cacela Velha, Loulé, Santa Bárbara de Nexe, Conceição, Vilamoura, Moncarapacho, Tavira, Alamancil, Estói, Santa Luzia, Quarteira, Fuseta, Luz de Tavira, Quinta do Lago, Olhão, Faro

Faro Old Town

Faro's venerable Cidade Velha (Old Town) is the city's most interesting quarter and can be appreciated at a leisurely pace on foot. Set within a circle of medieval walls, the whole vicinity is a veritable time capsule reflecting Faro's brief "golden age" in the 16th century. The landmark cathedral and cloistered convent are set alongside a patchwork of narrow, cobbled streets with some inviting cafés and shops. (For Faro's New Town see pp10–11.)

Igreja de Sao Francisco

🖝 The 16th-century Porta Nova in the south wall is near the embarkation point for Ria Formosa trips *(see p55).*

Cathedral entry includes access to the belltower, which offers spectacular views of Faro.

🖝 The bar-restaurante Aqui D'El Rei, on Rua do Repouso, is next to the little chapel of Nossa Senhora do Repouso.

Map K6 and town map at back of book • Tourist office by harbour (289) 803 604 • Museu Arqueológico open 10am–7pm (6pm winter) Tue–Fri, 11:30am–6pm (10:30am–5pm winter) Sat & Sun • Adm • Igreja de São Francisco open 8:30am & 6:30pm Mon–Sat, 9am & 6:30pm Sun

Top 10 Sights

1. Sé (Cathedral)
2. Museu Arqueológico
3. Igreja de São Francisco
4. Paço Episcopal
5. Arco da Vila
6. Nossa Senhora do Pé da Cruz
7. Nossa Senhora do Repouso
8. Galeria de Arte Arco
9. Galeria de Arte Trem
10. Walls and Towers

Sé (Cathedral)
The interior of the 13th-century cathedral *(right)* reveals a fusion of the Gothic, Renaissance and the Baroque: the Capela de Nossa Senhora dos Prazeres, especially, is a jewel of Baroque art, with splendid gilded and lacquered woodcarvings, inlaid marble and a surround of polished *azulejos*.

Museu Arqueológico
Gargoyles in the shape of animals embellish the delightfully secluded Renaissance cloisters of this former convent which imaginatively incorporates the museum. Highlights include a huge Roman floor mosaic, a collection of Moorish oil lamps and an exquisite 16th-century eucharistic safe. *(See p44.)*

Igreja de São Francisco
Stunning *azulejos* panels depicting the life of St Francis adorn the walls of this 17th-century church. The vault contains an outstanding polychrome panel showing the coronation of the Virgin.

Paço Episcopal
The original building was plundered and damaged by the Earl of Essex in 1596. Rebuilt again after the 1755 earthquake, it's still in use today, but closed to the public.

Arco da Vila 5

The grandiose arch *(left)* was inaugurated in 1812. Tucked inside the arch is an 11th-century horseshoe gate, which is believed to have been built by the Moors and is the only one of its kind in the Algarve.

Nossa Senhora do Pé da Cruz 6

Overlooking a pretty square, this 17th-century chapel is home to a lovely configuration of gilded wood carvings and a series of whimsical oil panels depicting scenes from the Old Testament. At the rear is a chapel with an 18th-century *azulejos* crucifix *(right)*.

Galeria do Arte Arco 8

Perched on top of the city walls, the Arco art gallery is worth a visit if only for its superb view of the Ria Formosa. A permanent collection of toys from the first half of the 20th century includes dolls, trains, planes and kitchen sets.

Galeria de Arte Trem 9

Housed off the main square and part of a former military barracks, the Trem art gallery shares floorspace with an excavated Roman arch built on Moorish foundations. The venue is a favourite among modern artists, both home-grown and visiting from abroad.

Walls and Towers 10

The original castle walls were Roman, vestiges of which can still be seen today. The rest of the fortifications are the result of 16th-century labour *(right)*. The exception is the Byzantine towers, added soon after the collapse of the Roman Empire and incongruous in their pentagonal design.

Nossa Senhora do Repouso 7

Set into a niche in the castle walls, this small chapel lies in the shadow of the medieval Gate of Rest. Popular legend has it that Afonso III, fresh from his victory over the Moors, rested here.

The Story of Faro

The Phoenicians and Carthaginians established trading posts on the banks of the Ria Formosa, which flourished into a major Roman port known as Ossonoba. The Moors fortified the town but couldn't halt the armies of Afonso III, who captured the city in 1249. A period of prosperity ended in 1596 when the Earl of Essex plundered and burned the city. Rebuilding began, but the 1755 earthquake destroyed it again, forever altering the urban makeup.

Left **Faro marina** Centre **Ermida de Santo António do Alte** Right **Tiles on the outer city walls**

Igreja do Carmo

Igreja do Carmo/ Capela dos Ossos

A feast of Baroque decoration, gilded with the finest Brazilian gold leaf. A macabre offering, though, is the Capela dos Ossos (Chapel of Bones), which is lined with the skulls and bones of more than a thousand monks.
Ⓢ *Largo do Carmo • Closed Sun • Adm*

Museu Marítimo

An engaging cruise around the Algarve's maritime heritage, from the Golden Age of Discoveries to the intricacies of catching tuna in the present day. *(See p45.)*

Teatro de Lethes

Once a Jesuit college, this little Italianate gem dates

from 1874 and is a beautiful example of a late 19th-century provincial playhouse. It hosts frequent plays, concerts and recitals. Ⓢ *Rua de Portugal 58 • (289) 820 300 • www. teatromunicipaldefaro.pt*

Science Alive Centre

An engrossing and highly original interactive study centre promoting scientific and technological awareness (all descriptions are in English and Portuguese). Climb up to the "observatory" for a voyage into the Milky Way.
Ⓢ *Rua Com. Francisco Manuel • Closed Mon • Adm • www.ccvalg.pt*

Museu Etnógrafico

Find out what rural Algarve looked like bereft of modern conveniences in this nostalgic display of sepia photographs, faded ceramics, kitchenware and dainty embroidered aprons.
Ⓢ *Praça da Liberdade • 10am–1:30pm, 2:30–6pm Mon–Fri • Adm*

Faro Jewish Heritage Centre

The city's 19th-century Jewish cemetery is laid out in the traditional Sephardic way. The adjacent Isaac Bitton Synagogue Museum is decorated with original 1820 furniture. Ⓢ *9:30am–12:30pm, 2–5pm Mon–Fri • www.farojewishheritage centre.org*

Teatro de Lethes

7 Ermida de Santo António do Alte

Built in 1355, this is one of the oldest buildings in Faro. A hop up the steps at the side of the chapel is rewarded with a fine city panorama. ❧ Rua da Merlim

8 Villa Romana de Milreu

Just 5 km (3 miles) north of Faro, Roman ruins at Milreu (see p84) include the remains of a luxury villa and baths dating from the 2nd century AD. ❧ Map K5

9 Ilha de Faro

A natural link in a chain of sand dune islands that constitute

Kite surfing, Ilha de Faro

part of the Parque Natural da Ria Formosa (see pp24–7), this is very popular in summer but near-deserted off-season. ❧ Map K6

10 Palácio dos Bívar

This late 18th-century former private residence is generally regarded as the finest example of Neoclassical architecture in the Algarve. ❧ Rua Conselheiro Bivar

---

Faro's Top 10 Personalities

1. **Mohammed ben Said ben Hárun** Gave Faro its name in 11th century.
2. **Afonso III** Captured city in 1249.
3. **Samuel Gacon** Produced first printed manuscript in Portugal (1487).
4. **Queen Catarina** Completed Convento de Nossa Senhora da Assunção.
5. **2nd Earl of Essex** Sacked Faro in 1596.
6. **Bishop Francisco Gomes** (1739–1816) Rebuilt city after quake.
7. **Francisco Xavier Fabri** (1761–1817) Architect.
8. **Manuel Bívar** (1861–1901) Prominent member of illustrious family.
9. **Dr Amadeu Ferreira de Almeida Carvalho** (1876–1966) Gave art collection to museum.
10. **Carlos Porfírio** (1895–1970) One of Portugal's greatest modern artists.

Cosmopolitan Faro

Statue of Bishop Francisco Gomes

Faro's history (see p9) and cosmopolitan flavour continues beyond the obvious Moorish and Christian features of the old town. New town houses sprang up outside the city walls in the 17th and 18th centuries, Mannerist in style. Battlements built during the War of Restoration (1640–68) enclosed this new urban area. Modernday Faro capitalizes on a vibrant social life and rich artistic heritage. Alluring historical buildings can be found alongside modern museums and quaint pavement cafés. The city boasts a colourful agenda of music, song and dance. As exciting, in fact, as the city's restaurants, where the best traditional cuisine of the Algarve can be sampled.

Light and airy café in Faro

🔟 Tavira

With its timeless atmosphere, traditional character and dignified charm, it's small wonder that many consider the elegant riverside town of Tavira to be the most pleasant and picturesque in the Algarve. Sited on both sides of the Rio Gilão, the town is perhaps best known for its abundance of churches – nearly 40 in all, with some dating back to the 13th century. The history of Tavira itself, though, is much older. Tavira's prosperity today relies to a great degree on tourism, although not to the detriment of the town's peaceful ambience.

Castle Remains
Crowning a cobble-stoned knoll, the surviving walls of this Moorish fort envelope a spruce garden. The view from the ramparts takes in the town's outline of pyramid-shaped rooftops to distant Ilha de Tavira. *(See p52.)*

Fishing boat

🤿 The Udiving Centre at Vila Galé Albacora *(see p127)* welcomes divers of all abilities. Call (936) 260 247.

Quatro Águas is lovely at sunset, but beware of mosquitoes near the river.

🍴 There are two cafés in Praça da República, near the Roman bridge. Charming Café Veneza has a pavement terrace and serves lovely fig cakes. Next door, the busy Romana serves light meals.

Map M4 and town map at back of book
• Tourist information Praça da República 5
• (281) 322 511
• Closed Sat & Sun
• Palácio da Galeria, Calçada da Galeria
• Map M4 • (281) 320 500 • 10am–12:30pm, 2–5:30pm Tue–Sat • Adm

Top 10 Sights
1. Igreja da Misericórdia
2. Igreja de Santa Maria do Castelo
3. Castle Remains
4. Convento da Graça
5. Ponta Romana
6. Torre de Tavira – Camera Obscura
7. Quatro Águas
8. Ilha de Tavira
9. Palácio da Galeria
10. Arabic-Style Lattice Doors

1 Igreja da Misericórdia
Townsfolk are justly proud that this 16th-century church is considered the Algarve's most important Renaissance monument. Its striking arched portal is surmounted by statues of saints.

2 Igreja de Santa Maria do Castelo
The clock face of this church is a familiar landmark *(below)*. Inside are the tombs of the Moors' nemesis Dom Paio Peres Correia and seven of his Christian knights.

Roman bridge (Ponta Romana)

4 Convento da Graça
Now a luxury *pousada (see p128)*, this grand 16th-century building is characterized by a rich mix of Baroque and Renaissance architecture, with the main attraction being the cloister. There are also the remains of a 12th-century Moorish street that can be seen from the bar lounge.

Ponta Romana

The foundations of the low, arched stone bridge spanning the Rio Gilão are Roman in origin. Illuminated at night in a romantic ethereal glow, the bridge is a favourite subject for artists.

Torre de Tavira – Camera Obscura

Housed at the top of an old water tower, the camera obscura focuses a live 360° image of the city onto a huge screen, with a guide on hand to point out the landmarks.

Quatro Águas

This beauty spot southeast of Tavira overlooks a sleepy lagoon and boasts some fine seafood restaurants. It is the jumping-off point for Ilha de Tavira. Quatro Águas is the name of the local style of rooftops.

Ilha de Tavira

A regular ferry service makes for an easy escape to the marvellous sand dune island, a popular resort during the summer months for its excellent swimming. It lies within the boundaries of the Ria Formosa nature park *(see pp24–7).*

Palácio da Galeria

Works by Picasso and Paula Rego have been exhibited at this first-class contemporary gallery, housed in a refurbished 16th-century palace. There is also an archaeological museum, with the glass floor of one room revealing an excavated street dating from around 1000 BC.

Arabic-Style Lattice Doors

Built into the façades of some of Tavira's back street properties are delightful examples of *portas de reixa* (lattice panelled doors; *right*). Arabic in design, each panel is made of finely interwoven lengths of wood. They evoke the Moorish influence still inherent in the region.

Local Cuisine

Tavira's seafood specialities include *acorda marisco,* a concoction of cockles, prawns and clams sunk in a thick bread-based soup, and *lulas cheias,* which is tender squid filled with cured meats and rice, and braised in an onion and tomato sauce. Santa Luzia, a village southwest of Tavira, is justly regarded the octopus capital of the Algarve. Order the octopus rice stew *(arroz de polvo).*

Silves

Known as Xelb in Arabic, the 30,000-strong Moorish settlement prospered until 1189 when Dom Sancho I laid siege to it with the help of an English crusader army. The Christians finally gained total control in 1242. These days, Silves is better known as a centre of citrus fruit and cork production. The castle, with its sandstone walls casting a sepia wash over the town below, is a stark reminder of Silves' once-powerful past.

Sé (Cathedral)

Dating from the 13th century, the town's Gothic cathedral was the seat of the Algarve see until 1580, when that honour was transferred to the bishops' palace in Faro. There are a number of curiosities to catch the eye, including petulant-looking gargoyles on the apse, and Crusader tombs.

Cathedral door

🔭 A pair of binoculars come in handy when scanning the countryside from the castle.

☕ The Café Inglês just below the castle is open daily for homemade fare. A rooftop terrace is open in summer.

Café Rosa, just off Rua 25 Abril, fronts a peaceful square and is decorated with *azulejos* panels.

Map F4 and town plan at back of book • Tourist information Parque das Merendes open Mon–Sat • (910) 762 385 • Museu Arqueológico open 10am–6pm Mon–Sat • Casa de Cultura Islámica e Mediterránica open 10am–1pm, 2–6pm Tue–Fri, 2–6pm Sat • Quinta do Francês Vineyard open Tue–Sun (Tue–Fri mid-Nov–mid-Mar)

Top 10 Sights

1. Castelo
2. Museu Arqueológico
3. Sé (Cathedral)
4. Casa de Cultura Islâmica e Mediterrânica
5. Quinta do Francês Vineyard
6. Cruz de Portugal
7. Arade River Cruise
8. Igreja da Misericórdia
9. Ponta Romana
10. Ancient Pillory

Castelo

The grandest monument to Islamic rule in the Algarve, Silves Castle is a stronghold of dynamic proportions, built on the site of 4th-century Roman fortifications. Views from the ramparts are superb.

Museu Arqueológico

An engrossing museum which superbly charts human existence in the region over the course of 8,000 years, from the Palaeolithic period to the mid-16th century *(see p44)*.

Casa de Cultura Islámica e Mediterránica

This interesting space in Largo de República promotes Silves' rich Islamic legacy and its links to Moorish and Mediterranean culture. It hosts temporary art exhibitions, and cultural events are held year round. For more details, contact the tourist office.

etc.

Quinta do Francês Vineyard

Set in a picturesque valley 6 km (4 miles) north-west of Silves, near Odeluca, this vineyard offers guided tours and tastings of award-winning reds, whites and rosés. Call (282) 106 303 to book. There's also a shop.

Cruz de Portugal

Standing rather incongruously next to a main road, the exquisite 16th-century granite cross *(above)* is said to have been a gift to the city from Dom Manuel I.

Arade River Cruises

The quay near the Roman bridge is where colourful sightseeing boats from Portimão stop (see p54). Look out for herons and flamingos. Departure times depend on the tide.

Igreja da Misericórdia

The highly decorative side doorway above ground level possibly served as the original entrance and shows the influence of the 16th-century "Manueline" style. The main chapel has a ribbed vault and Renaissance altarpiece.

Ponta Romana

Only the foundations of this pretty whitewashed bridge date back to Roman times. The rest of the structure is medieval in origin. These days it's closed to traffic, but not long ago the bridge was the only access point across the River Arade.

Ancient Pillory

A common symbol of municipal power across Portugal, the pillory standing near the castle was rebuilt from 16th-century remains. Topped by a decorative crown with four sinewy wrought-iron dragons jutting out from the stem, it is the only such example of its kind in the Algarve.

Moorish Silves

As Xelb, Silves was the capital of the Moorish province of Al-Gharb and by 1053 was a crowded metropolis. Writers, poets, scientists, lawmakers and philosophers lived here, and the shadows of several minarets fell across docks, a shipyard, public baths, a synagogue and church. By the mid-12th century, however, Silves started to decline. Nonetheless, the legacy of 500 years of Moorish rule can still be seen in the local architecture, fields of orange, almond, fig and carob trees, and in the Portuguese language itself.

The Algarve's Top 10

15

ᵀᵒᵖ10 Monchique

This spruce and engaging little market town nestles in the Serra da Monchique, a densely wooded canvas of eucalyptus, chestnut, pine and cork trees interrupted by tracts of barren moorland. A welcome change from beaches and villas, Monchique is all about cobbled streets and rural sentiment. The local medronho – firewater distilled from the berries of the arbutus (strawberry tree) – is the finest available anywhere.

2 Nossa Senhora do Desterro

A mysterious air pervades the ruins of the Franciscan monastery. Severely damaged by the 1755 earthquake, its empty shell echoes to the rustle of leaves from an immense magnolia (possibly the biggest in Europe) standing in the old garden. The interior is closed to the public.

Monchique town centre

🕊 For a pleasant walk, follow the terraced footpath in the grounds of the spa complex.

Monchique is also known for its small wooden "scissor" chairs, which neatly fold up between use and make good gifts *(see p98)*.

🍴 Reasonably priced cafés and restaurants cluster round the central bus station.

Down in Caldas de Monchique, Café-Restaurante 1692 has a marvellous terrace that spills out onto the square.

Map E3 • Tourist info office Largo S. Sebastião • Mon–Fri • (282) 911 189 • Galeria Santo António open Tue–Fri & Sun

Top 10 Sights

1. Igreja Matriz
2. Nossa Senhora do Desterro
3. Galeria Santo António
4. Caldas de Monchique
5. Termas de Monchique
6. Fóia
7. Parque Damina
8. Igreja de São Sebastião
9. Picota
10. Barranco de Pisões

View from the Peak of Fóia in the Serra da Monchique

3 Galeria Santo António

This engaging art gallery, housed in a former 18th-century hermitage, holds exhibitions of work by local and international artists, as well as live music events.

1 Igreja Matriz

An intriguing Manuel-ine doorway *(above)* greets visitors to Monchique's 16th-century parish church. The twisted columns resemble lengths of gnarled rope. Inside, the capitals of the columns in the three naves are similarly fashioned, suggesting a nautical theme.

5 Termas de Monchique

The delightful thermal spa complex is set under a canopy of pine and eucalyptus. Though modern, it retains a pleasant, bygone air *(see p124)*.

4 Caldas de Monchique

The Romans were bowled over by this cosy hamlet in the Monchique hills and totally enamoured by the hot, curative properties of its waters *(above)*.

6 Fóia

For the most stunning landscape views in the entire Algarve, head for the peak of Fóia. At 902 m (2,959 ft), this is the highest point in the Serra de Monchique.

7 Parque da Mina

Centred around a disused iron-ore mine, this imaginative theme park features a lovingly restored 18th-century manor house and a traditional distillery. There is also a nature trail, with shady picnic areas along the way *(see p57)*.

Monchique's Spa

According to legend, if you take a sip from the fountain of love, an ancient font hiding in the dappled woods behind Caldas de Monchique, you'll fall in love with life. The waters are said to be good for a whole host of maladies including rheumatic and digestive disorders and skin complaints. The Romans certainly thought so, as did Dom João II. Today's visitors are offered a range of water-based therapy, using vapours, water jets, hydromassage, steam and hot algae.

8 Igreja de São Sebastião

The church *(right)* contains a beautifully sculptured 17th-century figure of Nossa Senhora de Desterro.

9 Picota

At 773 m (2,536 ft), this second peak doesn't quite command the same all-round vista as Fóia, but Picota is steeper and pleasantly wooded. Its location affords beautiful views that take in long sweeps of scented meadows and a sparkling, distant sea.

10 Barranco de Pisões

A captivating little beauty and picnic spot about 4 km (2 miles) north of Monchique, the hideaway is known locally for its ancient waterwheel and 1,000-year-old plane tree.

TOP 10 Loulé

The pleasant inland town of Loulé is renowned for its traditional handicrafts and splendid market. The Romans first settled on the spot now occupied by the castle, but it was the Moors for whom Loulé was to become a conurbation of some importance. Remnants of their presence are still manifest in the belltower of Igreja Matriz de São Clemente, formerly a minaret. The castle is also Moorish in origin. Almonds and figs have been essential to the local economy for centuries.

Capela Nossa Senhora da Conceição
This delightful 16th-century chapel is decorated with *azulejos* and has a stunning Baroque altarpiece. The 19th-century ceiling panel is by Loulé painter Rasquinho.

Largo de Cargo, Roundabout

🔑 When the Islamic bathhouse is closed, ask for the key at the archaeology office at Rua Vice Almirante Cândido Dos Reis 36; (289) 400 642.

🏛 The pedestrianized Rua de 5 Outubro has plenty of bars and cafés, and is lined with shops selling traditional goods including foodstuffs, lace, woodwork and art.

For a more traditional setting, order a *bica* (small coffee) at Café Calcinha, Praça da República, 67.

Map J4 • Market Praça da República 7am–2pm Saturday
• Tourist office: Avenida 25 de Abril, 9 (289) 463 900
• Loulé Carnival in Feb (Shrove Tuesday)

Top 10 Sights

1. Castelo
2. Museu Municipal
3. Igreja Matriz de São Lourenço
4. Capela Nossa Senhora da Conceição
5. Market
6. Museu dos Frutos Secos
7. Igreja Matriz São Clemente
8. Galeria de Arte Convento Espírito Santo
9. Banhos Islâmicos
10. Loulé Carnival

Loulé Market

Castelo
The ruins underwent restoration during the 19th century and today the castle houses a museum. Visitors are rewarded with grand views of the town from its battlements *(see p52)*.

Museu Municipal
The best attraction of the museum *(right)* is the first-floor recreation of a traditional Algarve kitchen with its 19th-century utensils and tableware. There are also Bronze Age ceramics. *(See p45.)*

Igreja Matriz de São Lourenço
About 8 km (5 miles) south-east of Loulé, at Almancil, Blue and white *azulejo* panels grace the walls of the chancel, nave and magnificent trompe-l'oeil cupola of this decorative church.

Market

Mixed herbs, cheeses *(right)* and red chilli peppers vie for the eye with sweet figs, marzipan cakes and golden honey. Elsewhere, kaleidoscopes of flowers, the freshest of fish, the ripest of fruit and a variety of genuine handicrafts make a visit here an unforgettable shopping experience.

Museu dos Frutos Secos

The highly original museum focuses on early harvesting methods for figs, carob and almond fruit. Built in homage to a local businessman.

Igreja Matriz de São Clemente

Loulé's Muslim faithful were once summoned to prayer from the balcony of the lofty belltower which originally served as a minaret. The *azulejo*-clad Capela de Nossa Senhora da Consolação and the Capela de São Brás's Baroque altarpiece are Christian highlights.

Galeria de Arte Convento Espírito Santo

GALERIA DE ARTE

The decorated and vaulted ceilings of this former convent provide a splendid if rather incongruous setting for the contemporary paintings, sculptures and conceptual installations on display inside. There are regular contributions from local and international artists.

Banhos Islâmicos

The well-preserved ruins of an Islamic bathhouse known as *hammam de Al-'Ulyà* can be admired from a public viewing platform above the foundations, which date from the 1200s.

Loulé Carnival

The biggest, brightest and rowdiest of the Algarve's carnivals. Costume-clad revellers shake, rattle and roll for three days and nights to hybrid Latin rhythm and African-style percussion.

Traditional Crafts

It was the inauguration of an artisans' fair back in 1291 that forged Loulé's reputation as a manufacturing centre. Many of the techniques used 800 years ago are still employed today. Ceramics are popular with tourists. In many local villages, women still pleat the leaves of dwarf palms to make hats, baskets and rugs; jute fibre is used to stitch pretty rag dolls. Saddlers tucked away in quiet hamlets supply harnesses for mules, and old wooden looms are used to produce shawls and blankets.

TOP 10 Lagos

Lively, colourful and cheerful, Lagos is probably the most popular resort in the Algarve. Its easy-going atmosphere nourishes a predominantly young crowd who are attracted to the resort's bargain-stacked shops, welter of bars and restaurants, some of the hippest nightlife on the south coast and, of course, close proximity to lovely beaches and cliffs. Punctuating this cosmopolitan hubris is a rich historical vein, a source of great pride to the local population.

Fortaleza da Ponta da Bandeira

Accessible via drawbridge, this squat, tidy 17th-century fortress was built to defend the harbour. Nowadays, its sturdy ramparts protect a small museum dedicated to the Age of Discoveries.

Cafés in the town centre

🛥 For a boat trip to the grottoes, embark from Avenida dos Desbrimentos, in front of the marina. This way you'll pass the beautiful Dona Ana beach.

☕ Cafés, bars and restaurants along the Frente Ribeirinha esplanade provide appetizing drinks and meals, as well as harbour-front views.

For sweet almond delicacies and Italian ice-cream, call in at Taquelim Gonçalves on the marina.

Map D5 • Museu Municipal, Rua General Alberto Silveira • 10am–5:30pm Tue–Sun • Adm • Tourist office (282) 763 031, Praça Gil Eanes • Open daily

Top 10 Sights

1. Igreja de Santo António
2. Fortaleza da Ponte da Bandeira
3. Museu Municipal
4. Town Walls
5. Ponta da Piedade
6. Praia de Dona Ana
7. Igreja de Santa Maria
8. Slave Market Site
9. Monte da Casteleja Organic Farm and Vineyard
10. Marina de Lagos

4km

150 yards / 0 metres

1 Igreja de Santo António

This 18th-century church *(above)* is a dazzling jewel in the Algarve crown. Its gilded and painted woodwork positively overflows with ebullience. Everything the Baroque age is famous for is here: double-chinned cherubs, mythical beasts and ripened fruit. Entry is via the Museu Municipal.

3 Museu Municipal

This wonderful and totally absorbing museum houses an extraordinary collection of artifacts and oddities, plus one or two national treasures *(see pp22–3)*. Of particular note are the Roman mosaics, the 1504 town charter, vestments embroidered in gold and a collection of intricately carved and hand-painted model fishing boats.

For highlights of the Museu Municipal **See following pages**

Town Walls

The foundations of the walls *(right)* date from Roman times, strengthened during Arab and Christian occupation. Restored in the 16th century, the best preserved section encases a Manueline window from which Dom Sebastião is said to have addressed townsfolk before going to Alcácer-Quibir *(see p23)*.

Ponta da Piedade

Parts of the dramatic headland, 3 km (2 miles) northwest of town, resemble a huge wedge of crumbling ginger cake. Standing beneath gnarled sandstone cliffs are towering outcrops of umber-hued rock, hiding a warren of caves and grottoes. A lighthouse crowns the promontory, a suitably romantic location for a sunset finale.

Praia de Dona Ana

The photographer's favourite, postcards bearing the image of this beach *(right)* have been mailed around the world. Wedged between cliffs in a small sheltered bay, Dona Ana is often said to resemble an ancient amphitheatre. The stalagmite-shaped cylindrical towers of sandstone rising out of the shallows could pass for Roman columns.

Igreja de Santa Maria

The town's parish church dates back to the 16th century, although much of what you see today was rebuilt in the 19th century. The church, however, still retains its Renaissance doorway complete with Doric columns and busts of São Pedro (St Peter) and São Paulo (St Paul) on either side of the archivolt.

PRACA DA REPUBLICA

5 3km
6 2km

Slave Market Site

The northeast corner of Praça Infante Dom Henrique *(above)* is the site of Europe's first slave market in the 15th century.

Monte da Casteleja Organic Farm and Vineyard

This estate promotes organic farming and produces fine wine. Just 4 km (2.5 miles) east of the city centre, the winery sits in rolling countryside where a traditional farmhouse serves as a wine-tasting centre. Call (282) 798 408 for tours (except November).

Marina de Lagos

With 462 pontoon berths for yachts up to 30 m (100 ft) long, this first-class marina enjoys an international reputation. Distinguished with several awards, including a European blue flag, it's also known for its range of bars, restaurants and cafés. Several coastal- and river-cruise companies are based here.

Left **Altar, Igreja de Santo António** Centre **External entrance to the church** Right **Cork carving**

🔟 Highlights of Lagos Museu Municipal

1 Igreja de Santo António

After entering the museum, it is worth taking time to appreciate the adjacent church. The 18th-century interior, with its fantastic excess of gilded Baroque carvings, is sumptuous and impressive, and its finery is a compelling sight as part of the museum tour.

São Gonçalo de Lagos

2 Foral Dado a Lagos (Town Charter)

In terms of historical value, the original is priceless (the exhibit is a facsimile). Conferred on Lagos by Dom Manuel I in 1504, the beautiful leather volume binds a manuscript written on parchment, with the opening page embossed with gold leaf.

3 Altar de Campanha

An extraordinary 17th-century mobile altar that was carried by Portuguese troops into the field and used for prayer between military engagements. A carved statue of St Anthony rests on top of the altar, which is inlaid with gold leaf.

4 Priest's Vestments

A number of fine examples are displayed in the Sacred Art wing of the museum, but the most outstanding garment is the one worn at the Mass attended by Dom Sebastião in 1578 before his disastrous incursion into Morocco. The robe is hand embroidered with gold.

5 São Gonçalo de Lagos

A delightful anomaly, the 18th-century statue of Lagos' patron saint is incorporated into the door of a cupboard used by the priests of the time to store their shoes and robes. Ask the custodian to open it up.

Artifacts in the entrance to Lagos Museu Municipal

6 Traditional Portuguese Boats

An impressive collection of 28 miniature boats skilfully carved out of wood and hand-painted by local artisan Arez Viegas. The models include barges, launches, fishing boats and

The official museum tour incorporates the adjoining Igreja de Santo António, which is a national monument

Portrait of Estevão Amarante (1936)

steamers. The prize exhibit is the frigate *D. Fernando II e Glória*.

7 Portrait of Estevão Amarante

The life-size portrait of the late Portuguese thespian Estevão Amarante (not always on display) is by Fernando Santos. As you walk past the image, the change in perspective appears to make Sr Amarante's left foot move with you – an eerie sensation indeed!

8 Senhora do Forte Model Village

Housed in the Ethnographic Hall is a remarkable labour of love: a huge scale model of an imaginary Algarve coastal town. Constructed with breathtaking attention to detail, it took Lagos resident Pedro Reis 5,300 hours to build over a three-year, seven-month period.

9 Cork Altarpiece

A mini masterpiece of cork whittling, this framed, three-dimensional retable was carved by Silves resident Francisco Figueiras in 1907. Brimming with fancy filigree, it's so delicate that it will seem almost to tremble under your very gaze.

10 Opus Vermiculatum Mosaic

The impressive, near-complete Roman mosaic was unearthed in 1933 by the museum's founder, Dr José Formosinho, near Budens, 10 km (6 miles) west of Lagos. Complementing it is a smaller but wholly intact example discovered at Abicada, 2 km (1 mile) east of Portimão.

Story of Lagos

Fortress entrance

Lagos has "welcomed" visitors ever since the Phoenicians and Carthaginians established settlements along the banks of its superb natural harbour well over 2,000 years ago. Under subsequent Roman occupation the town became known as Lacobriga and flourished as a busy port. The ever-cautious Moors built a double ring of ramparts around its centre, but that was not enough to repel the Christians who conquered the city in 1241. During the 15th century – the period of Portugal's Golden Age of Discoveries – Henry the Navigator's caravels departed Lagos shipyards bound for far-flung African climes, and the town quickly became a centre for trade in ivory, gold, silver and other exotic merchandise. A far more unsavoury enterprise was also spawned…slavery! In 1578, Dom Sebastião bade Lagos farewell before heading off to Alcácer-Quibir, only to perish on the Moroccan battlefield along with 8,000 of his hapless troops. Lagos became the capital of the Algarve in 1576 and remained so until 1756 when the honour was transferred first to Tavira and then finally to Faro. By that time, however, much of the Algarve, Lagos included, lay in ruins after the devastating 1755 earthquake.

The harbour

Parque Natural da Ria Formosa

The Parque Natural da Ria Formosa comprises an extensive lagoon area that follows 60 km (37 miles) of coastline between Manta Rota and Vale do Lobo. Made up of sand dune islands, marshland, saltpans and shimmering freshwater lakes, the habitat provides sanctuary for an astonishing assortment of flora and fauna, including birds such as white storks and the rare purple gallinule. The park headquarters are at Quinta de Marim, 3 km (1.5 miles) east of Olhão.

Quinta do Lago Nature Trail
A partly shady trail *(above)* which highlights the flora of two widely differing ecosystems: woodland and marsh. The path winds past umbrella and maritime pines.

San Lorenzo (see p46)

⚙ Wear a pair of stout walking boots if you are planning to follow the nature trails, and put on warm clothing in winter.

Photographers in the hides will need a telephoto lens of at least 300 mm.

○ The Vista Formosa restaurant opposite the park's main entrance serves fresh grilled fish.

Map K–L6 • Quinta de Marim • (289) 700 210 for info about volunteering and conservation projects • Park open 9:30am–6:30pm (5:30pm in winter) Mon–Fri, 10am–6:30pm (5:30pm winter) Sat & Sun • Ecoteca Museu João Lucio • (289) 700 940 • Open 9:30am–12:30pm, 2:30–5:30pm daily

Top 10 Sights
1 São Lourenço Nature Trail
2 Quinta do Lago Nature Trail
3 Olhão Nature Trail
4 Freshwater Lagoons and Hides
5 Coastal Conifer Woods
6 Recuperation Centre for Birds
7 Tide Mill
8 Roman Salting Tanks
9 Coastal Dunes
10 Ecoteca Museu João Lucio

São Lourenço Nature Trail
One of the most rewarding introductions to the reserve is to follow the 3.2 km (1.8 mile) São Lourenço nature trail *(below)*. It will bring you into close contact with two different types of wetland: the salt marshes and the freshwater lagoons.

Coastal dunes

Olhão Nature Trail
The longest trail in the reserve meanders past a tide mill, the remains of Roman salting tanks and several wildlife observation hides before looping back to the park's headquarters.

4 Freshwater Lagoons and Hides

The freshwater lagoons provide vital refuge for nesting and migrating birds, and harbour a miscellany of aquatic mammals. The view from the observation hides *(right)* brings this sparkling marine oasis into sharp focus.

5 Coastal Conifer Woods

Coastal conifer woodland is sparse in the eastern Algarve, but where it occurs it provides an efficient means of coastal protection and adds to the diverse beauty of the terrain.

6 Recuperation Centre for Birds

This innovative hospital for sick and injured birds allows visitors (by prior arrangement) to observe the recuperating "patients", including birds of prey, via closed-circuit TV.

7 Tide Mill

A late 13th-century invention, tide mills were once very common in the lagoon and river estuaries along the Portuguese coastline. Power was obtained by utilizing the change in water levels associated with shifting tides. The example on the Ria Formosa *(below)* is the last of 30 that used to operate.

10 Ecoteca Museu João Lucio

João Lucio, 19th-century poet, lawyer and former mayor of Olhão, owned much of the land on which Quinta de Marim is now situated. His former villa, near the river's edge, is now an eco-museum *(below)*.

9 Coastal Dunes

The sweeping tracts of sand guarding the mouth of the estuary constitute a fragile environment, partly held together by the vegetation that has colonized them.

8 Roman Salting Tanks

Five Roman salting tanks *(above)* can be explored near the freshwater lagoons. Dating from the 2nd century AD, they were once used for salting fish prior to their distribution all over Rome's empire.

Left **Purple gallinule** Right **Rugged coastal terrain of the Ria Formosa**

Animals of the Ria Formosa

1 Purple Gallinule
Very rare, this striking bird is reclusive in nature and tends to play hide-and-seek in cattail that sprouts along the edge of the freshwater lagoons. A dark-coloured relative of the moorhen, there are just 20 couples in residence.

2 Portuguese Water Dog
Mild-mannered and intelligent by nature, this web-footed canine is unique to Portugal and one of the earliest known breeds in the world. A superb diver, the dog has won long-standing affection with the fishing community and with the general public.

Portuguese water dog

3 Mediterranean Chameleon
This is a treat indeed for anyone lucky enough to spy one of these remarkable creatures, wrapped as it is in a colour-co-ordinated skin. Hibernating from December to March, the best time to see this bulbous-eyed reptile out and about is on early spring mornings.

4 Greater Flamingo
There's no more majestic a sight than a pink band of flamingo panning for food on the salinas. Large flocks of these graceful birds gather in the park during autumn en route to winter breeding grounds, but they can also be spotted in the summer.

Greater flamingo

5 European Pond Terrapin
A whimsical little member of the chelonian family, this diminutive amphibian is fond of lakes, ponds and calm rivers. It is usually only detected as it darts for shelter through the water at the sound of approaching feet. Tread lightly!

6 Azure-Winged Magpie
A handsome, cheeky bird frequently heard chattering in small groups among the pine-woods near Quinta do Lago. Easily recognized by its sooty crown and nape, the blue flash of its wing feathers makes this species particularly alluring in flight.

7 Hoopoe
An exotic-looking bird with a lovely salmon-pink crest, the hoopoe is the golfer's companion, often seen probing for cutworm on the manicured

Pond terrapin

grass of fairways across the Algarve. Primarily a summer visitor, some individuals remain in the region throughout winter.

8 Fiddler Crab
Often seen scuttling in panic across the mud at low tide, the male of the species has one of its pincers (left or right) considerably more developed than the other. Its European distribution is confined wholly to the Iberian peninsula.

9 Viperine Snake
The Great Pretender, this snake is distinguished by its zig-zag dorsal line and chestnut-

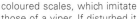

Fiddler crab

coloured scales, which imitate those of a viper. If disturbed it will rear up, inflate its neck and spit. But it's all theatrics – the snake is completely harmless.

10 Little Tern
The little tern's favoured nesting site in Portugal is along the Ria Formosa but the fact that it nests on the sand means that breeding is, at best, precarious.

Top 10 Plants in the Park

Dunes
1 Marram grass (helps support the dune)
2 Sea holly (top of dune)
3 Thrift (centre of dune)
4 Sea daffodil (delicate white flowers in summer)

Coastal Woodland
5 Furze (thorny shrub)

Salt Marsh
6 Cord grass (endures long submersion)
7 Sea lavender (identified by spikes of white, pink or mauve flowers)
8 Sea purslane (lance-shaped leaves and purple flowers)

Freshwater Lagoon
9 Cattail (cylindrical spike)
10 Rush (ideal shelter for aquatic wildlife)

Preserving the Environment

Want to spend more time at Ria Formosa and help preserve it for future generations? The Centro de Educação Ambiental de Marim (Marim Environmental Educational Centre – CEAM) works to protect the environment and promote a balanced and sustainable development of the park's natural resources. It runs a number of conservation projects manned by enthusiastic volunteers, and members of the public are welcome to join in. If you want to be involved in the coastal clean-ups, irrigation work and general maintenance of the park, call (289) 700 210. Some members of staff speak English. The park prefers volunteers who can commit to several weeks' work rather than just a few days. Note that there is no accommodation, and meals are not provided.

Lagoon, Parque Natural da Ria Formosa

...n summer with tassel-haired ...d with surfboards and a joie de ...harbour town is an excellent base from which to explore the fine beaches spread along the Algarve's untamed west coast. The sand-blown town itself is compact and crammed with welcoming pensões and residenciais (bed and breakfast accommodation). This is the most south-westerly community in continental Europe, and the sense of isolation is a major part of its appeal.

Fisherman on Sagres harbour

🕑 There are fine views of the promontory and Fortaleza de Sagres from the Ponta da Atalaia and the Praia da Mareta.

🍴 Try Dromedário bistro-bar on Rua Infante Dom Henrique for a mid-morning bite, or Café-Rest-aurante Cochina on Praça da República. On the road to Cabo de São Vicente, Waza Bar has tasty home-made snacks and is a meeting point for ornithologists.

Map B6 • Tourist information office is about 1 km (0.5 mile) from the fishing harbour at Rua Comandante Matoso
• (282) 624 873
• Closed Sat–Sun

Top 10 Sights

1. Fortaleza de Sagres
2. Nossa Senhora da Graça
3. Rosa dos Ventos
4. Ponta de Sagres Panoramic Walk
5. Parque Natural do Sudoeste Alentejano e Costa Vicentina
6. Cabo de São Vicente
7. Fortaleza do Beliche
8. Fortaleza da Baleeira
9. Farol de São Vicente
10. Menhir Circuit

Nossa Senhora da Graça
The foundations of this graceful 16th-century chapel are said to have been laid by Prince Henry the Navigator *(see box)*. Its whitewashed form faces Cabo de São Vicente.

Crab pots, Sagres harbour

Fortaleza de Sagres
Ominous, stark and in its time virtually impregnable, the massive front walls and two solid bastions are the impressive features of this 18th-century fort *(above; see also p53)*. Little else resembles a defensive structure today, except for the mighty cliffs themselves.

Rosa dos Ventos
The extraordinary giant wind rose, or wind compass – a device used for measur-ing the direction of the wind – is believed to have been built for Prince Henry *(see box)*. An impressive 43 m (141 ft) in diameter, the outline of the intriguing circle and its radiating points have been marked by pebbles *(below)*.

4 Ponta de Sagres Panoramic Walk

A bracing walk can be enjoyed round the edge of the promontory. Next to the lighthouse is a vast blow hole where you can hear the pounding of the ocean as it crashes into the rocks far below.

5 Parque Natural do Sudoeste Alentejano e Costa Vicentina

This park's wild and beautiful boundaries encompass nearly the entire western Algarve's rugged coastline and serve to protect a complex ecosystem. The area also lies under a busy migratory flight path and is popular with bird-watchers and voracious peregrine falcons *(see also p92)*.

6 Cabo de São Vicente

The forbidding look of this windblown cape is quite awe-inspiring. Greek historian Strabo, writing at the time of Christ, believed it to be the end "of all the inhabited earth", and its austere cliff face seems to encourage such thoughts *(see also p91)*.

7 Fortaleza do Beliche

Perched vertiginously on a pinnacle overlooking the Atlantic Ocean, the 17th-century fortification Fortaleza do Beliche also hugs a small chapel, which in turn marks the site of an even earlier ruined church, Igreja de Santa Catarina.

9 Farol de São Vicente

The tidy buildings surrounding this lighthouse *(farol)* incorporate a small museum, snack bar and gift shop. The tower is closed to the public but the fortifications afford majestic views of the coastline.

8 Fortaleza da Baleeira

A crumbling wall and arch *(below)* are about all that remain of the harbour fortification, but the coastal view from the headland is superb.

10 Menhir Circuit

Starting near Hortas do Tabual, this 2-km (1-mile) circular walk passes a series of *menhirs*, or megaliths, monumental stones that date back to 3000 BC.

Henry the Navigator (1394–1460)

Brooding, scholarly and devout, Prince Henry brought together the most learned of astronomers and astrologers, skilled cartographers and geographers, and the very best boat designers to create a school of navigation known as Vila do Infante. He oversaw and sponsored many a perilous expedition, and his vision and dedication eventually mapped the way for Portugal's "Golden Age of Discoveries".

⌐⌐10 Albufeira

Albufeira is one of Portugal's most popular holiday destinations and the largest resort in the Algarve. Famed for its fabulous beaches and exhilarating nightlife, the town gets very busy in summer when it positively bursts with energy. Its history is just as animated, from Roman settlement 2,000 years ago, Arab and Christian conquest in the 8th and 13th centuries, respectively, its rise and fall as a centre of trade and the emergence of its fishing industry.

Praia da Oura
Albufeira's "Golden Beach" sweeps the toes of the village-resort of the same name, giving it the advantage of proximity to shops and cafés.

The café-lined streets of Albufeira

⊘ Albufeira is at its most colourful during the Festa da Ourada, a delightful festival in mid-August that takes place on the beach in honour of the patron saint of fishermen.

⊘ Albufeira is awash with bars and cafés, but particularly appealing are those lining Largo Cais Herculano. Try out Cabana Fresca, right in front of Praia dos Pescadores, for their seafood snacks and chilled wine. Tasca do Viegas is another good choice.

Top 10 Sights

1. Praia dos Pescadores
2. Praia da Oura
3. Igreja de São Sebastião
4. Museu Arqueológico
5. Capela da Misericórdia
6. Adega do Cantor Vineyard
7. Castle Walls
8. Marina de Albufeira
9. Galeria Pintor Samora Barros
10. "The Strip"

Map G5 • Tourist Information office on Rua 5 de Outubro 8 • (289) 585 279 • Adega do Cantor open Mon–Fri (exc Christmas/New Year period) • (968) 776 971

Praia dos Pescadores

Igreja de São Sebastião
The altarpiece is the shining star of this exquisite church *(below)*. Its gilded form presides over a 14th-century statue of Nossa Senhora da Orada clutching a baby Jesus.

Praia dos Pescadores
"Beach of the Fishermen" is so-named because of the many small fishing vessels left stranded on the sand between use. The grizzled fishermen who own the boats seem oblivious to the sunbathers who descend on this well-known beach in summer.

Museu Arqueológico

Peer closely and you'll spy some charming exhibits: Roman earrings; a pair of Moorish scissors; and a near-mint 7th-century Visigoth earthenware wine goblet. *(See p45.)*

Capela da Misericórdia

This is Albufeira's oldest building of note *(below)*. Built in Gothic style in the 1500s, the chapel has since undergone many a stylistic change of heart.

Adega do Cantor Vineyard

Owned by British singer Sir Cliff Richard, this vineyard lies 6 km (4 miles) north-west of Albufeira, behind the Algarve Shopping mall *(see p60)*. Guided tours include tutored tastings, which are held in the well-stocked shop.

Castle Walls

The mighty ramparts that once surrounded Albufeira crumbled to dust as the 1755 Earthquake struck. A corner wall, the North Door, does survive though, in Rua Joaquim Pedro Samora. So does a remnant of St Anne's Gate, which forms part of a restaurant interior today.

Watersports

The crystal-clear waters of the Atlantic afford the Algarve a thriving water sports scene. At its simplest, fun begins with the humble pedalo, but for the more sea-hardy a diving centre (www.easydivers.pt) at Marina de Albufeira is great for beginners. For kids, the Leãozinho pirate ship (www.dreamwavealgarve.com) explores the nearby grottoes. Praia da Galé, about 6 km (4 miles) west, is known for its jet- and water-skiing, while windsurfers make for Praia da Falésia where fresh winds make it a favoured launch pad for paragliders.

Marina de Albufeira

The Algarve's fourth marina, 4 km (2.5 miles) west of the resort, is the departure point for sightseeing cruises, diving expeditions and fishing excursions. It also has its own holiday apartments and cheerful cafés lining the esplanade.

Galeria Pintor Samora Barros

Named in honour of the artist/poet whose diligent handiwork adorns the church, this airy gallery *(right)* overlooking the town square stages work by contemporary Portuguese and international artists.

"The Strip"

Glitzy, gaudy and totally irresistible, this is Albufeira's mini Las Vegas: a narrow, neon-lit runway of hotels and restaurants, pubs, cafés and dj-bars, with the odd *artesanto* (craft shop) squeezed in. Two of the region's top nightclubs, Kiss and Liberto's, hold court here.

For more on Albufeira's attractions and nightlife **See pp 62, 71, 77, 80 and 81**

Vila Real and Castro Marim

The original fishing village of Vila Real de Santo António was wiped out at the beginning of the 17th century by a momentous tidal surge. It wasn't until 1773 that Vila Real regained a place on the map. The town's reconstruction was overseen by the Marquês de Pombal (1699–1782), and under his eye the new town was planned and built, making use of a unique grid system. The town attracts day-trippers from Spain, and visitors can easily take in nearby Castro Marim, too.

Arquivo Histórico Municipal
An imaginative glimpse into Vila Real's past is seen in a free exhibition (Mon–Fri) on the region's almost vanished sardine and tuna canning industry.

Colourful houses, Vila Real

 When searching for Reserva Natural do Sapal (281 510 680) en route from Castro Marim, look out for a sign on the right on a tarmac road with "Reserva Natural" written in white letters on brown.

 Café Cantinho do Marquês, Praça Marquês de Pombal, 24, is a cheerful and accommodating bar which looks out onto Vila Real's central square.

*Map P3–4 • Castro Marim is 5 km (3 miles) north of Vila Real • Vila Real Tourist Information, Avenida Marginal, Monte Gordo
• (281) 544 495
• Closed Sat & Sun
• Castro Marim Tourist Information, Rua José Alves Moreira 2/4
• (281) 531 232
• Closed Sat & Sun*

Top 10 Sights
1. Praça Marquês de Pombal
2. Arquivo Histórico Municipal
3. Igreja Matriz
4. Espaço Manuel Cabanas
5. Castelo de Castro Marim
6. Núcleo Museológico
7. Former Igreja da Misericórdia
8. Fortaleza São Sebastião
9. Reserva Natural do Sapal
10. Centro de Interpretação do Território

Praça Marquês de Pombal
Vila Real's handsome central square is named after its creator, the Marquês de Pombal, and features a boldly graphic black and white mosaic pavement radiating from a central obelisk. The square is lined by a row of orange trees, which bear plump fruit, and a number of tidy 18th-century town houses, cafés and restaurants.

Praça Marquês de Pombal

Igreja Matriz
The highpoint, literally, of a visit to this church *(below)* is its six gorgeous stained-glass windows, set aloft over the chapel and altar. They were designed and installed by Algarvean artist Joaquim Rebocho as part of a major restoration in 1949. A further set at ground-floor level floods the baptistery with a surreal rainbow glow.

4 Espaço Manuel Cabanas

Dedicated to Portugal's foremost wood engraver of the 20th century, this museum shines a spotlight on Cabanas' extensive portfolio of ink-relief images of diverse subjects. *(See also p45.)*

5 Castelo de Castro Marim

This frontier stronghold *(above)* has two fortifications. The inner part, built by Dom Alfonso III in the 13th century, became headquarters of the Order of Christ. Dom João IV added outer ramparts in the 17th century *(see p52).*

6 Núcleo Museológico

Tucked inside the weatherworn battlements of Castro Marim castle is a humble museum, renovated in 2007, displaying a collection of local finds, including ancient lances, chipped cannon balls, ceramic fragments and amphorae.

7 Former Igreja da Misericórdia

Replaced many years ago by a much larger church situated outside the castle walls, the original 17th-century church *(above)* has still kept its looks thanks to generous restoration work. It is only open to the public during occasional exhibitions and for other cultural events.

The Salt Industry

Traditional saltworks like those near the centre of Castro Marim are made up of shallow reservoirs, or pans. Set below sea level, the pans are sub-divided into small ponds called *talhos*, into which salt water flows. The water evaporates in the heat of the sun, and the salt crystalizes. The process is repeated over a number of weeks until enough has been deposited. It's then removed onto the mud walls (*barachas*) that divide each pan, where it is collected into huge pyramids, for the most part using manual labour.

8 Fortaleza São Sebastião

Mirroring Castro Marim's castle from an adjacent hill, this larger fort, built for Dom João IV in 1641, is sadly only open to the public during the Medieval Fair *(see p58).*

9 Reserva Natural do Sapal

This large expanse of marsh and salt pans is an important breeding ground for plovers, avocets and black-winged stilts *(above)*. Flamingos may also be seen here. *(See also p83.)*

10 Centro de Interpretação do Territorio

The contemporary visitors' centre (open daily, with café) charts Castro Marim's heritage through a video presentation and interactive map. The windmill outside is a local landmark.

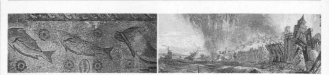

Left **Roman fish mosaic** Right **Painting of the Great Earthquake of 1755**

Moments in History

1 3000 BC: Early Peoples and Trade

Stone burial chambers (dolmens) and *menhirs* are characteristic of this period. By 1000 BC, Phoenicians have established sizeable trading stations. The Greeks also come, but their trade links are severed by the Carthaginians who blockade the Straits of Gibraltar and in 550 BC found the city of Portus Hannibalis (Portimão).

Menhir of Almendres

2 218–202 BC: Second Punic War

The Romans defeat the Carthaginians, then sweep through the Iberian peninsula. During the next 400 years, grand Roman cities and luxurious villas sprout up.

3 AD 415: Visigoths

After the fall of the Roman Empire the reins of power are seized by the Visigoths, a formidable warrior caste from eastern France and Germany.

4 711: The Moors Arrive

Internal strife and persecution among the Visigoths ultimately leads to one faction appealing for aid from Muslim North Africa. A large army of Berbers and Arabs conquers huge swathes of the Iberian peninsula. The Moors dominate the Algarve for well over 500 years, giving the region its name, al-Gharb, and turning Silves into an intellectual hub of staggering opulence.

5 Christian Crusades

Though Christians reconquer central Portugal in the 12th century, the Algarve is still firmly under Moorish rule. Dom Sancho (1185–1211) briefly takes Silves in 1189, but the city is recaptured by Al-Mansur. Dom Sancho II (1223–48) later launches a campaign to invade southern Portugal with the help of northern European Crusaders.

6 Portugal is Born

Faro is the last Moorish stronghold to fall, in 1249. Portuguese sovereignty over the Algarve is confirmed in a treaty with the kingdom of Castile in 1297.

Henry the Navigator

7 Era of the Great Discoveries

The Algarve plays a pivotal role in Portugal's maritime expansion in the 15th century. Henry the Navigator is made governor of the Algarve in 1418 and initiates the voyages

34

Tanks rolling in during the 1974 coup

of discovery from his bases in Sagres and Lagos. By the time of his death in 1460, Madeira, the Azores and Cape Verde islands have been discovered and much of the west coast of Africa has been mapped. In 1488 Bartolomeu Dias rounds the Cape of Good Hope, and ten years later Vasco da Gama opens the trade route to India.

Artistic Extravagance
The discovery of gold and diamonds in Brazil during the reign of Pedro II (1683–1706) later finances a period of great artistic extravagance under João V, who rules until 1750.

Great Earthquake of 1755
The quake devastates Lisbon and much of southern Portugal and plunges the nation into long-lasting crisis. Napoleon's troops invade in 1807.

Republicanism and Integration with Europe
The late 19th century witnesses political strife, with Republicanism taking root. António de Oliveira Salazar becomes prime minister in 1932, and turns around a stagnating economy but with the sacrifice of democracy. The army overthrows the government in 1974 in a near-bloodless coup. On 1 January 2002 the country adopts the euro currency.

Myths and Legends

1 The Moorish King and the Nordic Princess
The mythical king planted 1000s of almond trees to convince the princess that the blossom was like the snow she was used to.

2 Henry the Navigator
Henry assembled the best nautical minds in an academy, but why is there no trace of it?

3 Curse of the Vixen
On stormy nights in the Algarve hinterland, the raucous bellows of a hideous beast can be heard.

4 Capture of Aljezur Castle, 1249
A maid might have prevented the capture, but mistook the attacking knights for Moorish defenders and failed to raise the alarm.

5 St Vincent
Cabo de São Vicente is associated with a 4th-century martyr, whose body was watched over by ten ravens.

6 Enchanted Cássima
The pitiful cries of a Moorish woman supposedly echo in the streets near Loulé Castle.

7 Hannibal and the Elephants
Legend has it that the great general landed at Portimão.

8 Manueline Window
King Dom Sebastião (1557–78) is said to have roused an army from the window at Lagos Castle.

9 Pot of Treasure
A pot full of gold coins lies on the road between Mexilhoeira Grande and Praia da Rocha. Kiss the toad guarding it, and the pot is yours.

10 The Cry of Aben Afen
Listen out for battle cries near Silves – the ghost of the city's last Arab lord.

Left **Sunbathers** Centre **Rocky outcrops, São Rafael** Right **Children, Praia da Rocha**

🔟 Beaches

1 Praia da Dona Ana, Lagos

A beautiful and intimate beach, caressed by clear waters and flanked by huge outcrops of mustard-red sandstone. Easily reached by car and public transport, and about 25 minutes' walk from the centre of Lagos. A nearby warren of coves and hidden grottoes is ripe for exploration by boat. ⊗ Map D5

2 Praia da Ilha de Tavira, Tavira

Ostensibly an elongated sand bar, Ilha de Tavira's windward side is a magnet for water sports enthusiasts. Leeward, opposite Tavira, the sheltered beach skirts a campsite and a string of cafés and fine seafood restaurants. There are two access points to this spit. From Pedras del Rei, you can walk across a causeway or catch a ride on a miniature railway. Alternatively, regular ferry boats depart from the jetty at Quatro Águas. ⊗ Map M5

3 Praia dos Pescadores, Albufeira

This hugely popular tract of sand is characterized by the colourful fishing boats stationed at one end – indeed, its name translates as "Fishermen's Beach". Right in front of the town's old quarter, the beach is reached through a tunnel next to the tourist information office. ⊗ Map G5

4 Praia do Armado, Carrapateira

Pummelled by Atlantic swells, Armado is one of Portugal's premier surfing venues, and its surf school enjoys international patronage. Sitting well off the beaten track, this west coast beach also attracts families, and the rock pools at low tide teem with inquisitive children. ⊗ Map B4

5 Praia da Rocha, Portimão

One of the most famous and impressive beaches in the Algarve, Praia da Rocha is one vast blanket of golden sand set against a backdrop of cliffs the colour of cinnamon. It can get very crowded in summer, but a tunnel at the western end allows access to narrower stretches of sand. At various points along Avenida Tómas Cabreira there is further access via steps, some of them steep. ⊗ Map E5

Praia da Dona Ana

Be aware of warning signs on some beaches, indicating hazardous cliff faces where rockfalls are a potential threat

Praia da São Rafael

6 Praia da São Rafael, Albufeira

With its shallow waters and soft white sand, Praia da São Rafael can fill up quickly. Its pretty bay is framed by some extraordinary rock formations, pocked by a number of caves just waiting to be investigated. It offers ideal snorkelling territory and is popular with families. ◈ Map G5

7 Praia de Odeceixe

One of the Algarve's best kept secrets, Odeceixe is in a spectacular setting, up in the northwest corner of the Algarve. Its sheltered, crescent-shaped beach is just a short drive (along a road that shadows the path of the river) from the quaint village of Odeceixe. Even in summer, the beach is always wonderfully uncrowded. ◈ Map C1

8 Praia da Marinha, Benagil

Steep steps hewn into rock lead down to two compact and secluded beaches tucked below soaring cliffs. A treat for snorkellers, Marinha is served by a small café. ◈ Map F5

9 Praia de Figueira, Salema

This select swathe of sand is popular with youngsters and windsurfers. There are also some excellent nearby dive sites, such as Boco do Rio to the east, where the wreck of the *Ocean*, an 18th-century French man-of-war, lies in shallow water. Praia de Figueira lies right in front of the village of Salema. Arrive early to find parking space. ◈ Map C5

Praia de Odeceixe

10 Meia Praia, Lagos

A giant curve of sand 4 km (2 miles) in length makes this the longest beach in the Algarve. There's plenty of room for water-skiing, windsurfing and jet-skiing and those seeking a little peace and quiet. It also makes for a lovely walk, especially in autumn when the summer hoards have begun to disperse. ◈ Map D5

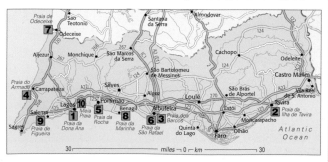

Left **Monte Gordo** Right **Carvoeiro**

TOP 10 Resort Towns

1 Lagos
Drawing the whole gamut of visitors, from backpackers, package tourists and wealthy expatriates, Lagos exudes a lively and inviting atmosphere. Modern amenities and historical sights make for an appealing mix of old and new, and the nearby coves, framed by russet and mustard rocky outcrops, are some of the most spectacular in the Algarve *(see pp20–21).* ✎ *Map D5*

2 Albufeira
Bright, loud and unashamedly extrovert, Albufeira buzzes with vitality in summer. Wide sweeping beaches, first-class water sport facilities and dozens of bars, bistros, restaurants and nightclubs lend the resort its non-stop party atmosphere, though the old quarter still manages to convey a mellow charm. *(See pp30–31.)* ✎ *Map G5*

3 Praia da Rocha
Some of the very first holiday hotels in the Algarve sprang up here back in the 1960s, and Praia da Rocha hasn't looked back since. Vibrant and engaging, this resort is famed for its outstanding golden beach. And at night, revellers dance till dawn in the clubs and bars that skirt the sand. ✎ *Map E5*

4 Vilamoura
Designed around a marina of international repute, this upmarket resort has championship golf courses, a stylish casino, luxury hotels and sumptuous villas. Fabulous cruises depart from the marina *(see p72).* ✎ *Map H5*

5 Alvor
Nestling in a sheltered bay midway between Portimão and Lagos, Alvor is an unusual mix of dignified charm and flickering

Albufeira

neon. The old quarter is a delight to wander through, the 16th-century Manueline church is a gem and the village restaurants serve up some of the tastiest seafood in the region. ✎ Map D4

Armação de Pêra

The beach here is one of the longest in the Algarve and fronts a commercial hub of tall, angular apartment blocks, seafront hotels and rows of cafés and bistro bars. But this is all rather functional, so instead everyone heads east for Pêra's livelier old town, spread around the site of a small fortress. ✎ Map F5

Carvoeiro

Friendliness suffuses this alluring little town, making it ideal for families. It is one of the Algarve's main self-catering areas, and the hilltops that flank the pocket-sized beach are awash with apartments. On the other side of the promontory is the snorkelling territory of Algar Seco rock formation. ✎ Map E5

Monte Gordo

A generous beach and a casino (popular with big spenders from Seville) are the twin targets for most visitors to this, the closest Algarve beach resort to the Spanish border. The esplanade is fringed by lofty

Armação de Pêra

palms and even loftier apartment blocks with fabulous views of the ocean. ✎ Map P4

Sagres

Though not strictly a resort town – it has little in the way of entertainment infrastructure and its isolated position keeps it off the tourist treadmill – Sagres offers access to some of the most unspoilt beaches in the Algarve. (See pp28–9.) ✎ Map B6

Quarteira

The brazen tourist hub that is Quarteira is home to a throng of holiday apartments near the beach. The remodelled fishing harbour is a hive of activity in the mornings, when returning boats deposit their glistening catch on the quayside, most of it destined for the town's market next door. ✎ Map H5

Left **View across the river from Alcoutim** Right **Caldas de Monchique**

🔟 Inland Villages

1 Alte

The town's cobbled streets, colourful window frames and cheerful chimney pots invoke an unhurried air that is quite disarming. Alte's church retains a fine portal and is situated near a leafy square. The spring running along its flank tumbles under an old mill, providing a favourite picnic spot. ◈ Map H3

2 Caldas de Monchique

The warm spa water here has brought visitors since at least the age of the Roman Empire. It is just as alluring today, but there are other reasons to visit this hillside hamlet, not least the wood of pine and eucalyptus which provides a lush, cooling canopy in the heat of summer. Woodsmoke and birdsong drift

Alte

lazily through a valley peppered with whitewashed cottages and smallholdings. ◈ Map E3

3 Alcoutim

The town's 14th-century castle keeps one timeworn eye on its townsfolk and the other on the old adversary, Sanlúcar, Alcoutim's mirror image on the Spanish side of the River Guadiana. The silence here is palpable, interrupted only by the chiming hour and the rattle of stork bills as they chatter to one another from church towers and chimney stacks. ◈ Map P1

4 Estói

Just off the town's main square is the Palácio do Visconde de Estói, a 19th-century Rococo palace (now a beautiful *pousada*), with gardens fanned by giant palms and cooled by fountains. A 20-minute walk from here brings you to Milreu (see p84), a Roman complex dominated by the apse of a temple that was converted into a Christian basilica in the 5th century. ◈ Map K5 • Milreu Tue–Sun • Adm

5 Salir

The walls of Salir's Moorish castle are lit up at night and emit an eerie glow, but on the other side of the village the view is more benign, stretching across the valley from the parish church and garden. In summer this rural idyll is blanketed by narcissi and alive with the warbling of brightly coloured passerines. ◈ Map J3

Paderne

Early in the 17th century the entire population of Paderne moved from the shadows of the nearby castle to the environs of a newly consecrated church. That village is now a sleepy place of faded charm and modest means, but therein lies its beauty. The architecture retains a certain grandeur, while the Moorish castle stands close by, still wondering where all the people went. ❧ *Map G4*

Querença

Best known for its 16th-century church and the ancient, weather-worn cross that stands at the southern edge of the village's picturesque square, Querença, surrounded by the Caldeirão mountains, is relatively isolated, which is part of its allure. ❧ *Map K4*

Guerreiros do Rio

The scenic road south from Alcoutim runs part way along the banks of the River Guadiana and passes through a landscape bristling with olive, fig and carob trees before reaching this tiny village. Amid the orange trees, a former schoolhouse now houses a modest museum providing a

Salir

glimpse into the history of the Guadiana River. ❧ *Map P2*

Martin Longo

The storks nesting on top of the belfry of Martin Longo's parish church have been members of this small community for years, and they are as appealing as their unusual home. But the "A Flor da Agulha" dolls workshop is also worth a visit, for it is here that traditional jute dolls are hand crafted, the figurines depicting ladies spinning, herdsmen and woodmen. ❧ *Map L1*
• *Workshop: Mon–Fri except hols*

LARGO DA IGREJA Nª Sra DA ASSUNÇÃO

Village sign, Querença

Barão de São João

Wrapped in classic hill-walking country and pleasantly lost in time, Barão de São João typifies rural Algarve. It is best appreciated during the antiques fair, which the village hosts on the last Sunday of every month. ❧ *Map C4*

Left **Fishermen's cottages, Cacelha Velha** Centre **Surfer near Arrifana** Right **Salema beach**

Coastal Villages

1 Cacelha Velha

The settlement is little more than a whitewashed church, a squat, 18th-century fortress and a row of fishermen's cottages, but it is quite exquisite and totally unspoilt. Fanned by an invigorating sea breeze, this smudge of antiquity looks out over a lagoon and the Atlantic beyond. It's a popular weekend destination for locals, who happily queue for the only restaurant *(see p89)*. 🖎 *Map N4*

2 Ferragudo

A maze of cottages, converted lofts and cube-like town houses tumble down towards the river and Praia Grande, a vast swathe of sand popular with sunbathers and windsurfers. The seafood restaurants lining the tidy quayside are some of the best in the Algarve. 🖎 *Map E5*

3 Santa Luzia

An old seafaring myth claims Santa Luzia came by its foreign-sounding name after an effigy of the Virgin Mary was salvaged from an Italian vessel. Today the image most associated with Santa Luzia is *covos* – octopus pots. This is the octopus capital of the Algarve, and hundreds of the earthenware pots, all numbered and roped together, can be found piled neatly on the beach in readiness for their next outing. 🖎 *Map M5*

4 Salema

Even if you're not staying in Salema, it's worth detouring to it from the EN 125, via the beautiful ravine, speckled most of the year with colourful flora and fleet-footed goats. The tarmac peters out where the cobbled slip road begins, a causeway cluttered with colourful fishing boats, rickety lobster pots and shrouds of netting. The sloping streets are banked with salt-laced terraced houses and cramped little tavernas. 🖎 *Map C5*

5 Burgau

The best time to savour the village-like atmosphere of Burgau is out of season. You notice more when the cobbled lanes are deserted and the only sound is the collision of the ocean with the beach. There are some lovely coastal walks, too, with many prime picnic spots. 🖎 *Map C5*

Santa Luzia

Odeceixe

The isolated splendour of this attractive hillside village makes the long drive north along the Algarve's western coast worthwhile. Odeceixe's beach, cut in two by the mouth of the Seixe creek, is the prize draw *(see p37)*. Late spring is the best time of year to visit, when it's warm and not too busy. ◈ *Map C1*

Carrapateira

This is where surfers come to relax after a day taming the waves at Praia da Bordeira and Praia do Armado *(see p36)*. A loose configuration of terraced cottages and sandblown cafés, Carrapateira is well used to the camper vans that disgorge the salt-encrusted youths. ◈ *Map B4*

Arrifana

Craggy, precipitous cliffs tower over Arrifana's superb beach and accompanying village, which looks as though it's about to be swallowed up by the

Odeceixe

Benagil

dunes. This is the west coast at its wildest and most desolate, attracting only die-hard surfers and those seeking solace with the elements. ◈ *Map B3*

Benagil

Benagil straddles a steep, narrow valley which ambles its way towards a bay the size of a postage stamp. More hamlet than village, Benagil is blessed with a couple of superb seafood restaurants positioned on the lip of the valley, with views across the ocean. ◈ *Map F5*

Luz de Tavira

It's one of those villages you normally drive through on your way somewhere else. But stop off to view the south door of the local church. The highly ornate portal is one of the loveliest examples of Manueline architecture in the Algarve. ◈ *Map M5*

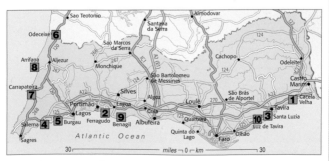

Left **Mosaic, Museu Arqueológico, Albufeira** Right **Roman ruins, Museu Cerro da Vila, Vilamoura**

🔟 Museums

1 Museu Municipal, Lagos
This highly entertaining ethnographic museum brings together a fantastic collection of oddities, rarities and priceless treasures *(see pp22–3)*.

2 Museu Arqueológico, Faro
Set within the cloisters of the former convent of Nossa Senhora da Assunção, this museum is one of the Algarve's most beautiful. Highlights include a giant Roman floor mosaic, fragments of a Moorish bowl inscribed with "Allah" and a gallery devoted to 16th-century Italian, Spanish and Portuguese paintings. ◙ *Largo Dom Afonso III • Map K6 • summer: 10am–7pm Tue–Fri, 11:30am– 6pm Sat & Sun; winter: 10am–6pm Tue–Fri, 10:30am–5pm Sat & Sun • Adm*

3 Museu Cerro da Vila, Vilamoura
A first-rate modern museum and historic Roman site, Cerro da Vila is an outstanding example of a 2nd-century villa complex, with sunken baths, salt tanks, a burial tower and brilliant black-and-white patterned mosaics. The adjacent museum houses a superb display of Roman, Visigoth and Moorish artifacts. ◙ *Cerro da Vila • Map H5 • May–Oct: 10am–1pm & 4–9pm daily; Nov–Apr: 9:30am–12:30pm & 2–6pm daily • Adm*

4 Museu Arqueológico, Silves
This excellent museum is unique in Portugal for its astonishing 12th-century Arab well-cistern. Unearthed by chance in 1980, it is the star exhibit around which the entire building is constructed. An original staircase (closed to the public) incorporated into the ancient structure descends 15 m (49 ft) to the bottom of the well. ◙ *Rua das Portas de Loulé • Map F4 • 10am–6pm daily (last adm 5:30) • Adm*

5 Museu Etnográfico do Trajo Algarvio, São Brás de Alportel
This delightful rural ensemble of local costumes, papier-mâché dolls, decorated carriages and

Left **Museu Arqueológico, Faro** Right **Museu Arqueológico, Silves**

Museu Etnográfico do Trajo Algarvio

traditional handicraft is aptly housed in a wonderful country mansion. Particularly poignant is a child's faded tunic and breeches displayed next to a photograph of one José Maria Féria wearing the same costume in 1929. ◉ *Rua Dr José Dias Sancho • Map K4 • (289) 840 100 • 10am–1pm & 2–5pm Mon–Fri, 2–5pm Sat & Sun • Adm*

Museu de Portimão

This superb museum charts the development of the region's local communities, in particular the fish-canning industry. Housed in what was once a cannery, displays include Roman and Moorish artifacts and the factory's former 19th-century cistern. ◉ *Rua D. Carlos I • Map E4 • (282) 405 230 • mid-Jul–end Aug: 3–11pm Wed–Sat, 7.30–11pm Tue; Sep–mid-Jul: 10am–6pm Wed–Sun, 2.30–6pm Tue • Adm*

Museu de Arqueológia, Loulé

Loulé's archaeological heritage is admirably chronicled with displays of Stone Age, Bronze Age and Roman artifacts. Upstairs, history is closer to the present day, with a reconstruction of a traditional Algarve kitchen, replete with 19th-century crockery and a worn *xarém*, or maizewheel. ◉ *7 Rua D. Paio Peres Correia • Map J4 • 9am–5.30pm Mon–Fri, 10am–2pm Sat • Adm (inc castle)*

Museu Marítimo, Faro

Carlos Porfírio's dramatic oil painting of wild-eyed fishermen drawing a huge net over a shoal of desperate, thrashing tuna overlooks this spirited exhibition of nautical paraphernalia. The scale models of caravels, galleons and steamboats are wonderful. ◉ *Rua da Comunidade Lusiada • Map K6 • 9am–noon & 2:30–5pm Mon–Fri • Adm*

Museu Arqueológico, Albufeira

The view from this modern museum looks out to the ocean, while inside is a modest but fascinating collection of Stone Age, Roman and Moorish artifacts. The 10th-century Arab silo is worth close scrutiny, as are the set of weathered 16th-century keystones. ◉ *1 Praça da República, Albufeira • Map G5 • 10:30am–4:30pm Tue–Sun (closed lunch Sat & Sun) • Free*

Espaço Manuel Cabanas, Vila Real de Santo António

A museum showcasing the work of Portugal's greatest wood engraver of the 20th century, Manuel Cabanas (1902–95). A truly dynamic volume of work is exhibited: ink-relief images of politicians, statesmen, writers and musicians, plus views of everyday rural life. ◉ *Avenida da República, Vila Real de Santo António • Map P4 • 9:30am–12:30pm & 2–4:30pm Mon–Fri • Free*

Museu Marítimo, Faro

Left **San Lorenzo** Centre **Le Meridien Penina Hotel** Right **Pinta Course**

🔟 Premier Golf Courses

1 San Lorenzo

In the Parque Natural da Ria Formosa and one of the top five golf courses in continental Europe. The par 72 layout culminates with a green on the 18th that must be approached from across a lake. Part of the Dona Filipa & San Lorenzo Golf Resort *(see p126)*, the course is open to visitors, with priority given to hotel guests. ⊗ *San Lorenzo Golf Club, Quinta do Lago • Map J5 • www.sanlorenzogolfcourse.com*

2 Sir Henry Cotton's Championship Golf Course

A par 73 layout designed by the great golf-course architect Sir Henry Cotton in the mid-1960s. Le Meridien Penina Hotel *(see p122)* overlooks the course, which stretches over parkland terrain, its sweeping fairways dotted by water hazards. Two of the great holes are the dogleg 5th, with its canal, lake and

Palmares

contoured green, and the alarming 13th, shadowed by water from tee to green. ⊗ *Penina, near Portimão • Map E4 • www.lemeridienpenina.com*

3 Quinta do Lago South

This par 72 championship course lying within the vast estate of the same name has hosted the Portuguese Open on several occasions. The undulating layout favours long hitters, but strategic bunkering, the odd water hazard and large, contoured greens provide challenge aplenty. ⊗ *Quinta do Lago Campo de Golfe, Quinta do Lago • Map J5 • www.quintadolago. golf.com*

4 Palmares

With the original 18-hole par 71 layout already a favourite among Algarve golfers, Palmares is now a 27-hole golf course thanks to an extra 9 holes that were added as part of a major resort development. The additional holes take full advantage of the spectacular coastal views afforded by verdant sloping fairways. ⊗ *Onyria Palmares Golf Resort, Lagos • Map D5 • www.onyriapalmares.com*

5 Royal Course, Vale do Lobo

A rolling terrain abundant with pine envelopes this par 72 layout. The highlight is the infamous 16th, where a powerful and accurate swing is needed to carry a set of precipitous cliffs before the green. But the signature hole is the 9th, with

Its spectacular, semi-island green. ❧ *Royal Golf Course, Vale do Lobo • Map J5 • www.valedolobo.com*

6 Oceânico Old Course, Vilamoura

A mature course of classic British design, opened in 1969 and still revered today. Endowed with mostly narrow, pine tree-lined fairways, the only lake is on the 4th, where the tee shot must clear not only the water but also a large pine and bunker hugging the green. ❧ *The Old Course, Clube de Golfe, Vilamoura • Map H5 • www.oceanicogolf.com*

7 Vale da Pinta Course, Pestana Carvoeiro

One of the layout's wonders is a stately olive tree, believed to be over 1,200 years old. In fact, most of the natural contours of this par 71 estate were retained to include the ancient tree life that characterizes this course. Pinta is home to the prestigious David Leadbetter Academy. ❧ *Pinta Pestana Golf & Resort, Carvoeiro • Map E5 • www.pestanagolf.com*

8 Pinheiros Altos

This 27-hole championship layout with demanding water features has three contrasting 9-hole formats – the Pines, the Corks and the Olives – each a par 36. The original 18 holes

Pinheiros Altos

were designed by the golf architect, Ronald Fream; the rest, by the architect, George Santana da Silva. ❧ *Pinheiros Altos, Quinta do Lago • Map J5 • www.pinheirosaltos.pt*

9 Parque da Floresta

Built on hilly coastal terrain, this challenging par 72 can be exposed to stiff breezes, so club selection can vary considerably in the unpredictable winds. Never more so than on the short 5th, which is played from hill-top to the crown of a hillock. ❧ *Parque da Floresta Golf Resort, Vale do Poço, Budens • Map C5 • www.parquedafloresta.com*

10 Oceânico Victoria

Designed by golf legend Arnold Palmer, this undulating 18-hole par 72 layout is regarded as one of the best and most sophisticated courses in Europe. It features wide fairways and extensive water hazards. ❧ *Hotel Tivoli Victoria, Vilamoura • Map H5 • www.oceanicogolf.com*

Left **Alto Golf** Centre **Benamor** Right **Vila Sol Golf**

🔟 Holiday Golf Courses

1 Vale de Milho
This superb 9-hole course is a test of a golfer's short game. A compact layout of interesting holes, the design encompasses ingenious water hazards and bunkers similar to those found on a full course. First-class service and amenities include a computerized swing analysis. ⬧ *Vale de Milho Golf – Praia do Carvoeiro, Carvoeiro • Map E5 • www.valedemilhogolf.com*

2 Alto Golf
With its sweeping views of the ocean, this splendid course was the last work of eminent designer Sir Henry Cotton. Over 10,000 trees were planted on the par 72 layout, attracting a wealth of colourful birdlife. Aside from the 604-m (nearly 2,000-ft) 16th, the course is not overly difficult. ⬧ *Quinta do Alto Poço – Alvor • Map D5 • www.altoclub.com*

3 Penina Academy Course
A compact, 9-hole course laid out amid the Championship fairways. The ease of play should relax even the most nervous of players, and the adjoining golf academy offers individual or group tuition. ⬧ *Le Meridien Penina Golf & Resort Hotel, Penina, near Portimão • Map E4 • www. lemeridienpenina.com*

4 Balaia
Popular with beginners as well as the more adroit, this layout is recommended for the holiday golfer who prefers a fairly relaxed game. It requires concentration, however, especially for club selection, as the holes vary in length more than one might expect of a 9-hole course. ⬧ *Balaia Golf Village, Sítio da Balaia, Albufeira • Map G5 • www.balaiagolfvillage.pt*

5 Benamor
A beautiful, rolling par 71 course, with widely varying holes and a mix of coastal and mountain views. The outward nine are relatively easy, but the back nine are trickier, particularly on the 15th and 18th, the latter with out of bounds areas on either side close to the green. ⬧ *Quinta de Benamor, Conceição, near Tavira • Map M4 • www. benamorgolf.com*

6 Vila Sol Golf
Originally a standard 18-hole course, a third 9-hole loop was

Vale de Milho

introduced, allowing for three combinations of 18 holes. The course features daunting water hazards and large, contoured greens. The club also has an excellent driving range and academy. ⊗ *Vila Sol Spa & Golf Resort, Morgadinhos, Vilamoura • Map H5 • www.pestanagolf.com*

7 Quinta da Ria

Bordering the Parque Natural da Ria Formosa, this par 72 layout affords the distraction of some spectacular ocean views. Amid olive and carob trees, some of the man-made lakes have now become home to many species of waterfowl. Elsewhere, greens skirt a vineyard and an orange grove. ⊗ *Quinta da Ria, Vila Nova de Cacela • Map N4 • www.quintadaria.com/golf*

8 Castro Marim

The excellent par 71 Atlantic Course commands glorious views across the River Guadiana and to Spain beyond. The layout features a number of lakes, undulating fairways and elevated greens, and has been designed to offer a challenging yet relaxing experience to golfers of all levels. ⊗ *Castro Marim Golfe and Country Club, Castro Marim • Map P3 • www.castromarimresort.com*

9 Gramacho Course, Pestana Carvoeiro

Gramacho gained another 9-hole layout to add to the original double 9, and the combination allows for a variety of options in pin settings and length to suit both high and low handicappers. ⊗ *Pestana Golf & Resort – Carvoeiro • Map E5 • www.pestanagolf.com*

10 Pine Cliffs

A spectacular clifftop layout, this 9-hole course is set against an ocean backdrop. The course hides under a canopy of umbrella pine, with narrow fairways demanding a steady swing. The final hole requires a shot from the "Devil's Parlour" clifftop tee that will carry a deep ravine to hit the green. ⊗ *Pine Cliffs Resort, Pinhal do Concelho, near Albufeira • Map H5 • www.pinecliffs.com*

Pine Cliffs

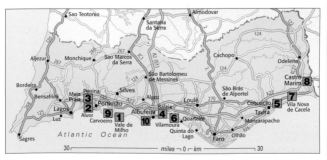

Left **Reserva Natural do Sapal nature trail** Right **Monchique-Fóia circuit**

⟲⟲ Walks in the Algarve

1 Parque Natural da Ria Formosa/São Lourenço, Quinta do Lago and Olhão Trails

Three one-hour nature trails reveal a rich coastal wonderland of salt marsh, woodland and freshwater lagoon. The winter months are very rewarding with huge flocks of greater flamingo and spoonbill mingling with pintail, gadwall and teal. The prize attraction, though, is the rare purple gallinule, a striking member of the coot family. ⊗ *Map J–L6*

2 Tavira National Wood (Mata Nacional)

Fine, panoramic views characterize an easy to moderate walk, the start/finish point of which is only accessible by car. The 8-km (5-mile) track snakes its way through beautiful rolling countryside, fording two small streams and passing the diminutive villages of Malhada de Peres and Daroeira. ⊗ *Map M4*

3 Monchique-Fóia-Monchique Circuit

The 11-km (7-mile) walk begins in the town square and takes in the ruins of a Franciscan convent. Shady woodlands echo in summer to nightingales and cuckoos, and are full of butterflies tumbling through the air. The ascent steepens before the cluster of antenna prickling Fóia's summit come into view. ⊗ *Map E3*

4 Burgau Coastal Walk

The spectacular clifftop paths between Salema and Luz are well-trodden by ramblers who enjoy negotiating headlands and don't mind the occasional stony track. The full distance is about 10 km (6 miles), but to halve that length, start the walk from Burgau. ⊗ *Map C5*

5 "Ilha" do Rosário, Silves

A serene circular walk which partly follows the course of an irrigation ditch *(levada)* and two rivers. The 8-km (4-mile) path begins at the Mira-Rio restaurant on the N124 where it picks up the *levada* before heading towards the "Ilha" do Rosário viewpoint. The path then veers through lush, open countryside and skirts a tiny hamlet, Vale da Lama, before meeting the restaurant again. ⊗ *Map F4*

Rocha da Pena, Penina circuit

For more guided and self-guided walks in the Algarve visit www.portugalwalks.com or www.viaalgarviana.org

Reserva Natural do Sapal Nature Trail

The trail is around 6 km (3 miles) in length and two hours in duration, although ornithologists can spend all day in bliss scanning the reedbeds and saltmarsh for plovers, avocets and other wading birds,

Benagil-Senhora da Rocha Clifftop trek

plus many species of duck and gull. During the summer, visitors can also observe the salt harvest. ◈ Map P4

Climb to Rocha dos Soidos, Alte

Combines exploration of Alte, arguably the prettiest village in the Algarve, with a hike to the summit of Rocha dos Soidos. The climb is long and steady rather than steep. It will take about three hours to complete the round trip which includes an alternative route of descent via Soidos de Baixo. ◈ Map H3

Esteveira Dune Walk

The fragile habitat of the dunes contains a wealth of flora, including the beautiful large yellow restharrow which blankets the sand with a bright mantle of delicate petals. ◈ Map C2

Penina Circuit

A real hike in the hills that will appeal to the experienced hill walker. The region is a protected area of outstanding natural beauty and bristles with aromatic lavender and rosemary. Native *cistus* species are the dominant shrubs. The walk passes two ancient defensive walls and the Cave of the Moors. ◈ Map J3

Benagil-Senhora da Rocha Clifftop Trek

Coastal erosion has eaten into the cliff face to produce some fantastic natural sculpture washed with a beautiful russet and mustard hue. The footpath, which is quite steep in places, looks over a series of delightful half-moon coves packed with golden sand. And there are ample spots to picnic in along the way. ◈ Map F5

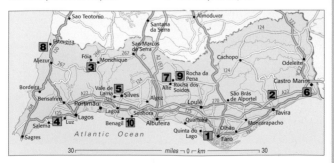

Left **Castelo de Castro Marim** Centre **Fortaleza Cacelha Velha** Right **Silves**

🔟 Castles and Forts

1 Silves
One of the Algarve's great landmark features, Silves Castle dates back to Moorish times, but may have been built on Roman fortifications. Its formidable red sandstone battlements and massive polygonal towers enclose a vast compound. ◈ *Map F4 • 9am–5:30pm daily (to 7pm in summer) • Adm*

2 Castelo de Castro Marim
The enormous frontier castle overlooks the border between Spain and Portugal. Built in the 13th century, the castle was the first headquarters of the Order of Christ. Henry the Navigator was a frequent visitor. ◈ *Map P3 • Apr–Oct: 9am–7pm daily; Nov–Mar: 9am–5pm • Adm*

3 Alcoutim
Enjoying a lovely setting, Alcoutim commands glorious views across the River Guadiana and the Spanish town of Sanlúcar. Built in the 14th century, it was here that the short-lived peace treaty between Fernando I and Henrique of Castile was signed on 31 March 1371. ◈ *Lago do Castelo • Map P1 • 10am–1pm, 2–7pm daily (to 6pm in winter) • Adm*

4 Loulé
The immaculately restored battlements are an integral part of the town's historical make up. A wonderful little museum has been built into the castle walls, including a recreation of a traditional Algarve kitchen. Grand views from the ramparts. ◈ *Map J4 • 9am–5:30pm Mon–Fri, 10am–2pm Sat • Adm*

5 Tavira
Only the walls remain of this old Moorish fortification which surround a charming, well maintained garden. There are lovely views. ◈ *Map M4 • 8am–5pm Tue–Fri, 9am–5:30pm (10am–7pm in summer) Sat, Sun and public hols, closed Mon • Free*

Alcoutim

Fortaleza de Sagres

The fortress is steeped in history and myth. Huge walls and bastions date from 1793: little, if anything, remains of Henry the Navigator's original fortress.

Aljezur

Whether or not there was an academy of navigation founded here remains a matter of debate and legend. An 18th-century sundial fashioned into the wall is aligned with the famous wind compass (see p28). ◊ Map B6 • 10am–6pm daily (til 8:30pm May–Sep) • Adm

Aljezur

Dominating the landscape around Aljezur are the ruins of the town's 10th-century castle. Perched on a hillock with fabulous views of the coast and Serra de Monchique, this Moorish stronghold controlled an ancient river port and provided a vital link with the open sea. Its broad, overgrown courtyard hides remnants of a vaulted cistern and is surrounded by high ramparts reinforced by two towers, one round, the other square. ◊ Map C3 • Free

Paderne

The atmospheric ruins of Paderne's long-abandoned Moorish castle are best appreciated on a Sunday morning, or early evening when the ramparts are illuminated. The thick outer walls of mud and sandstone and the remains of a barbican tower are all that exist of the original structure. Inside, the chapel of Nossa Senhora da Assunção lies in mournful pieces. ◊ Map G4 • Free

Fortaleza Cacelha Velha

This pocket-sized fortress sits in the quaint hamlet of Cacelha Velha, 8 km (5 miles) west of Monte Gordo, in the eastern Algarve. Polygonal in shape, the building dates from the 18th century and overlooks a gentle lagoon teeming with waterfowl. Its squat turrets are topped with whitewashed cones. ◊ Map N4 • Closed to public

Salir

The ruins of Salir's Moorish castle have been put to novel effect by locals who have sunk gardens in between the battlements and the keep. The rest of the structure can be explored by treading a circular path around the middle of the fortifications. A small museum completes the picture. ◊ Map J3 • Free

Left **Colourful livery on the Bom Dia** Centre **Riosul Guadiana** Right **Rio Arade river boat**

TOP10 Coastal and River Cruises

Schooner Condor de Vilamoura

Condor de Vilamoura
Choose a trip to Albufeira's coastal grottoes or a cruise with beach barbecue at Armação de Pêra. ⚓ *Cais I, 25, Marina de Vilamoura • Map H5 • (289) 314 070 • Mid-Mar–Nov • www.condordevilamoura.com*

Caravela Santa Bernarda
This replica of a 500-year-old Portuguese caravela charts caves and grottoes between Lagos and Armação de Pêra. ⚓ *Rua Júdice Fialho 11, Portimão • Map E4 • (967) 023 840 • Feb–Nov • www.santa-bernarda.com*

Bom Dia
This colourful schooner sets sail for the Ponte de Piedade grottoes, where dinghies allow closer inspection of this natural wonder. ⚓ *Marina de Lagos, 10 • Map D5 • (282) 087 587 • Mid-March–mid-Nov • www.bomdia.info*

Seafaris
Claiming an 80 percent success rate, this semi-inflatable powers out of the marina. When dolphins are sighted, it reduces speed and waits for a display of marine antics. ⚓ *Seafari Stand, Marina de Lagos • Map D5 • (282) 798 727 • www.seafaris.net*

Riosul Guadiana
A trip along the Guadiana, passing the Reserva Natural do Sapal. Lunch at Foz de Odeleite and music and wine on return. ⚓ *Rua Tristão Vaz Teixeira, 15, Monte Gordo • Map P4 • (281) 510 200 • Every Tue, Thu (& Sun May–Oct) • www.riosultravel.com*

Rio Arade
This ancient waterway allows for an absorbing journey to Silves *(see pp14–15)*, where

Left **Caravela Santa Bernarda** Right **Schooner Bom Dia**

Cruising on the Rio Arade

you can explore for an hour before the return. ◈ *Esplanade, Portimão • Map E4 • (914) 983 967/(967) 474 791 • www.rivertriptosilves.co.uk*

Ilha Deserta Cruise

A maritime expedition through the waterways of the Parque Natural da Ria Formosa, possibly the best way to explore this diverse wetland. Lunch is at O Estaminé, which specializes in seafood. ◈ *Porta Nova Wharf, Faro • Map K6 • (918) 779 155 • www.animaris.pt*

Ria Formosa

Hop onboard a traditional fishing boat and meander through the myriad channels and lagoons of the Parque Natural da Ria Formosa, watching a wealth of birdlife at close quarters. ◈ *Marina de Faro, Faro • Map K6 • (918) 720 002 • www.formosamar.pt*

San Lorenzo Champagne Cruises

Enjoy a flute of champagne as you step aboard this luxury motor yacht that also has a jet ski tucked away in the stern. ◈ *Marina de Vilamoura, Q11 • Map H5 • (965) 656 675 • www.champagnecruises.net*

Leãozinho "Pirate Ship"

The "Captain Hook" cruise takes kids and parents past São Rafael, Castelo and Galé beaches and some truly magnificent rock formations. ◈ *Escritório MT1, Marina de Albufeira • Map G5 • (289) 102 117 • www.dreamwavealgarve.com*

Top Ten Algarve Sporting Activities

Surfing
Surfers from around the world converge on the west coast beaches, notably Praia do Armado and Praia da Arrifana.

Windsurfing
The Atlantic westerlies, especially at Praia da Salema and Praia do Matinhal, are a treat for windsurfers.

Horse Riding
Through the countryside or over a bracing coastal path, riding a Lusitano horse is a joyful way to explore the land.

Game Fishing
Fishing expeditions depart from resorts and marinas throughout the summer in search of marlin and shark.

Scuba Diving
Sea caves, historic wrecks and a wealth of marine life await those who don wetsuit and aqualung and plunge into the Algarve depths.

Walking and Hiking
Guided walking tours take in rolling hills, mountain gullies and exhilarating coastal ranges.

Tennis
The Algarve's many tennis academies provide ample opportunity to better your game.

Sailing
The warm waters off the Algarve provide a natural arena for all type of sailing craft, from dinghy to schooner.

Cycling and Mountain Biking
Cycles can be hired if you wish to explore at your own pace and off the beaten track.

Kite Surfing
Local surf schools have everything you need to get started in the Algarve's latest radical watersport.

Left **Krazy World Zoo** Centre **Karting** Right **Zoomarine**

🔟 Children's Attractions

Zoomarine
1 Promoting conservation and environmental education, Zoomarine has seal and sea-lion shows, tropical birds and bird-of-prey presentations – and you can swim with dolphins. A water slide, fun fair, and "4D" cinema are among the attractions. ◈ Estrada Nacional 125, Guia • Map G5 • Mid-Mar–Oct: 10am–6pm daily (to 7:30pm Jul–Aug) • Adm • www.zoomarine.pt

Aqualand – Algarve
2 Head first or feet first, dare to disappear down one of the huge tubular water chutes and you will find yourself twisting and turning in spiralling loops to be discharged with a huge splash into a vast swimming pool below. This is one of Europe's biggest open-air waterparks and is set in a landscape of shady palms and trim gardens with lots to do between getting dunked.

Lagos Zoological Park

◈ Estrada Nacional 125, Alcantarilha • Map F4 • Jun: 10am–5pm Sun–Fri; Jul & Aug: 10am–6pm daily; Sep: 10am–5pm daily • Adm • www.aqualand.pt

Krazy World Zoo
3 Snakes and alligators are among the residents at this highly entertaining animal park. The pet farm is sanctuary to smaller, more cuddly creatures. Kids can enjoy pony rides, play a round of mini-golf or have fun in the inflatable playground.
◈ Lagoa de Viseu, near Algoz • Map G4 • 10am–6pm daily (winter hours vary) • Adm • www.krazyworld.com

Aquashow Family Park
4 The Water Roller Coaster at this outstanding theme park is the only one in Portugal and the biggest in Europe. It's a white-knuckle ride to remember. Other favourites are the White Fall and Wild Snake water chutes. Toddlers can paddle in Waterland, where the playground is in the swimming pool. ◈ Semino, near Quarteira • Map H5 • May–Sep: daily • Adm • www.aquashowpark.com

Lagos Zoological Park
5 A menagerie of exotic wildlife. Bushy-tailed lemurs, sure-footed gibbons and rotund Vietnamese pigs share the grounds with graceful flamingos, leggy emus, beady-eyed toucans and bouncing wallabies. ◈ Estrada Municipal de Bensafrim, Barão de S. João • Map D4 • 10am–5pm daily (to 7pm in summer) • Adm • www.zoolagos.com

6 Almancil Karting

Experience life in the fast lane at this challenging circuit, an exact replica of the Jacarepágua Formula 1 track in Brazil. There are smaller circuits with less powerful machines for kids. ✪ *Vale d'Éguas, Almancil • Map J5 • Feb–Dec: 10am–6pm Tue–Sun (from 2pm Tue); summer hrs vary • Adm • www.kartingalgarve.com*

Slide & Splash

7 Family Golf Park

Two 18-hole mini-golf courses test the skills of children and parents alike. Catch the tourist train that tours Vilamoura before returning for refreshments at the café. ✪ *Rua dos Marmeleiros, Vilamoura • Map H5 • (289) 300 800 • Feb–Oct: from 10am daily (closing times vary) • Adm • www.romagolfpark.com*

8 Slide & Splash

Corkscrew, Black Hole and The Tornado are some of the best water chutes. The adrenaline rush starts working overtime when you're halfway down the Kamikaze water slide. ✪ *Parque de Divertimentos Aquáticos, Estrada 125, Vale de Deus, Estômbar, Lagoa • Map E4 • Apr–Oct: 10am–5:30pm daily (to 6pm in summer) • Adm • www.slidesplash.com*

9 FIESA Sand Sculpture Festival

The Algarve's international sand sculpture festival brings together some of the world's most talented artists. The huge sculptures are illuminated at night. Also features performing arts and shows. ✪ *E524, between Pêra and Algoz • Map F4 • mid-May–mid-Oct: 10am–9pm daily (to midnight Jun–Sep) • Adm • www.fiesa.org*

10 Parque da Mina

An adventure theme park and heritage centre all rolled into one. With advanced booking, the energetic can traverse a lofty rope slide, and for younger children there is an attractive playground. Visitors can learn about the old iron-ore mine and explore an 18th-century manor house. ✪ *Sítio do Vale de Boi, Caldas de Monchique • Map E3 • (962) 079 408 • Mar–Oct: 10am–7pm Tue–Sun (5pm Oct) • Adm*

Left **Fatacil, Lagoa** Centre **National Folklore Festival, Alte** Right **Popular Saints Parade, Quarteira**

TOP 10 Festivals

1 Fatacil, Lagoa
The premier showcase for all things Algarve, this nine-day jamboree attracts visitors from all over Portugal. It is part agricultural show, part handicrafts fair – with a music concert, trade exhibition and gastronomy festival thrown in for good measure. ⬙ *Fatacil showground, EN 125, Lagoa • Map E4 • Mid-Aug • Adm*

2 Algarve Classic Car Festival
Hundreds of legendary and collectible sports cars can be seen at this annual event. Various races take place for different categories of vehicle. Previous events have attracted celebrated drivers such as Sir Stirling Moss. ⬙ *Autódromo Internacional do Algarve, Mexihoeira Grande • Map D4 • 3rd weekend Oct • www.autodromodoalgarve.com • Adm*

3 Medieval Fair, Castro Marim
Towards the end of the summer the town of Castro Marim returns to the Middle Ages to host a spectacular pageant in the grounds of the 13th-century castle. Archers draw their bows on mocking bullseye targets while mounted knights tilt their lances and jesters cajole the crowd with music and banter. At night, actors in period costume recreate medieval plays to a hushed audience. ⬙ *Castro Marim • Map P3 • 31 Aug–2 Sep • Adm*

4 Festival Med, Loulé
This highly regarded world-music festival celebrates Mediterranean and North African culture through a series of concerts, art exhibitions and culinary events in and around Loulé. It also includes world-class acts from Brazil, the Caribbean and sub-Saharan Africa. Many of the town's historic monuments – such as the castle and Islamic bathhouse *(see pp18–19)* – serve as suitably inspiring venues for the festival. ⬙ *Loulé • Map J4 • Last week in Jun*

Folk musician

5 National Folklore Festival
The entire Algarve becomes an impromptu stage as lively troupes of dancers and singer-musicians from across Portugal descend on the region for two weeks of spirited performances. It is a celebration of centuries-old culture, an insight into the charming and diverse world that is Portugal's folklore heritage. ⬙ *Various regional venues • Mid-Sep*

6 Mãe Soberana, Loulé
This is the Algarve's most important religious festival, linked to ancient maternity rites. On Easter Sunday, a 16th-century statue of Mãe Soberana (the Sovereign Mother) is carried into town from her hilltop shrine. Exuding solemnity and piety, the

subdued procession makes its way to Loulé's parish church where the image rests for two weeks. On the return journey the mood is more ebullient – flowers are tossed at the cortège, and the air rings with cries of "Viva Mãe Soberana". ◈ *Loulé town centre • Map J4 • Usually last week Apr*

Silves Medieval Fair

Silves returns to its former medieval splendour during this remarkable festival. The historic centre's narrow streets and alleys become one huge souk. Visitors can enjoy colourful processions, live music, street theatre and jousting competitions. ◈ *Silves • Map F4 • Last week Jul–1st week Aug • Adm for jousting displays*

Portimão Sardine Festival

Generally regarded as the sardine capital of the Algarve, Portimão throws a big party in summer to honour this venerable fish. Hungry revellers are drawn to the riverfront by the delicious aroma and live music. On the last night, there is a huge fireworks display. ◈ *Portimão riverfront • Map E4 • Approx 2nd week Aug*

Popular Saints Parade, Quarteira

The resort town of Quarteira celebrates Portugal's popular saints – St Anthony, St Peter and

Mãe Soberana, Loulé

St John – on three separate nights in spectacularly colourful style, when its townsfolk parade in traditional costume along the main boulevard. Thousands gather to watch the spectacle, which is full of fun, music and laughter. ◈ *Marginal de Quarteira • Map H5 • 12, 23 & 28 Jun*

Seafood Festival, Olhão

Olhão is the Algarve's biggest fishing port, and at festival time numerous stalls groan under the weight of every imaginable seafood delicacy, including octopus, squid, clam, prawn, mussel and the ubiquitous grilled sardine. Folk music and dancing add further flavour. ◈ *Jardim Patrão Joaquim Lopes, Olhão • Map L5 • 10–15 Aug*

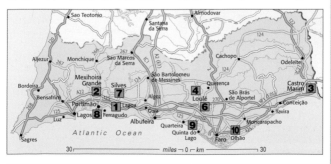

Left **Quinta Shopping** Right **Loulé market**

Shopping Malls and Markets

1 Forum Algarve, Faro

Created with much more than shopping in mind, Forum Algarve is the biggest mall of its kind in the whole region, attracting visitors and residents alike. More than 200 shops, boutiques and department stores, as well as an enormous hypermarket, multi-screen cinema and family entertainment centre are imaginatively incorporated into an architectural design inspired by Faro's historic city centre. ✆ *Forum Algarve, EN 125, Faro • Map K6 • 10am–midnight daily*

2 Algarve Shopping, Guia

The exterior of this shopping complex is striking in its colour scheme, following the geometric pattern of traditional Algarve architecture. Inside, the mall

Algarve Shopping, Guia

boasts more than 130 stores, 45 fashion boutiques, a hypermarket and food hall. ✆ *EN 125, Guia • Map G4 • 10am–midnight daily*

3 Quinta Shopping, Quinta do Lago

The elegant mall with its open-air terraces and wide esplanades is situated within the exclusive Quinta do Lago estate. Well-known fashion houses showcase their latest ready-to-wear designs. Top-range jewellery, cosmetic and perfume stockists also have a presence. ✆ *Quinta do Lago, Almancil • Map J5 • 9am–10pm daily*

4 Loulé Market

On Saturday mornings this market bursts with the freshest harvest from the ocean and the hinterland. Delicate sprigs of herbs and spices hang over pots of honey and jam. Cakes made from fig and almond compete for space with loops of smoked sausage, fresh fish glisten and everywhere it seems are blooms of bright flowers. ✆ *Praça da República, Loulé • Map J4 • 9am–2pm Sat*

5 Aqua Portimão

Centrally located, this modern shopping mall features nearly 80 shops and boutiques and a huge hypermarket. There are several ATMs, and underground car parking is free. The top floor is all restaurants. ✆ *Rua de São Pedro 72, Portimão • Map E4 • 9am–11pm daily (to midnight Fri, Sat, Jul, Aug, Dec)*

Apolónia Supermarkets, Almancil & Guia

Shoppers in the know travel here from right across the length and breadth of the region. Foreign produce such as fresh Argentinian beef, macaroni pasta and spicy tandoori curry powder feature. The cosmopolitan wine selection includes bottles from California, Chile and Australia. ✎ *271 Avenida 5 de Outubro, Almancil & Sitio Vale do Rebelho, Guia • Map J5 • 8am–8pm daily*

Quarteira Fish Market

One of the best-loved fish markets in the region, where the catch is landed at dawn and on sale by 8am. Be prepared to haggle. Note that the throng is usually greatest around the famous Quarteira prawns. ✎ *Largo do Peixe, Quarteira • Map H5 • 7am–1pm daily*

Armação de Pêra Fruit & Fish Market

This colourful indoor and outdoor market has an amazing choice of fresh fruit and fish, including crab, lobster and clams. Outside you'll find jams, honey and tongue-tingling *piri-piri*. ✎ *Behind Largo da Igreja, Armação de Pêra • Map F5 • 7am–1pm Mon–Sat*

Porches Pottery

The blue and white façade of the building is unmistakable, and the pottery produced here is

Forum Algarve, Faro

equally striking. Rows of women gossip merrily amongst themselves while deftly applying a final lick of paint to the latest batch of crockery. ✎ *Porches, Lagoa, EN 125 • Map F4 • 9am–6pm Mon–Fri, 10am–2pm Sat*

Olhão Market

Situated right on the esplanade overlooking the lagoons, this is a fantastic place to shop for fresh fish, fruit and vegetables and flowers. A riot of noise and colour takes place under two purpose-built pavilions. On Saturdays it is enlivened by extra stalls selling anything from basketware and smoked sausage to honey and lace. ✎ *Avenida 5 de Outubro, Olhão • Map L5 • 7am–2pm Tue–Fri, 6:30am–3pm Sat*

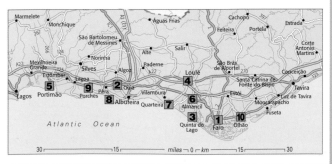

Left **Nosoloagua, Portimão** Centre **"The Strip", Albufeira** Right **Stevie Ray's Blues Jazz Bar, Lagos**

🔟 Clubs and Late-Night Bars

1 Kiss, Albufeira
Arguably the most famous of all the Algarve nightclubs, Kiss is known for its memorable party nights and zany theme festivals. Three dance floors reverberate to cutting-edge house, techno and hip-hop, attracting seasoned clubbers from all over the continent. Kiss starts to smoulder around 3am and is still sizzling at dawn. ⚘ *Areias de São João, Albufeira • Map G5 • Midnight–6am daily in summer*

2 Kadoc, Vilamoura
A sprawling venue of gargantuan proportions, the nightclub can accommodate up to 7,000 party-goers on five dance floors illuminated by a spectacular tricolour laser system. The clientele is young and energetic. A landscaped open-air terrace set in a tropical garden offers a great spot for those chill-out sessions. The last club to wind down, closing around 7am. ⚘ *Estrada de Vilmoura • Map H5 • From midnight Sat, Sun, Mon • "Kadoc Club" from midnight Fri, Sat, Sun, Mon • www.kadoc.pt*

Kiss, Albufeira

3 Nosoloagua, Portimão
Located right on the beach, this chic bar/restaurant is a favourite summer hangout for a young, fashionable crowd. Live-music nights feature an eclectic range of styles, from blues and bossa nova to traditional jazz and fado. Guest DJs spin tracks on Saturday nights. Sunset parties take place around the swimming pool and continue after dark. Entry is free until 1am. ⚘ *Marina de Portimão–Praia da Rocha • Map E5 • Daily in summer*

4 Liberto's, Albufeira
One of the must-see nightclubs, rivalling Kiss in popularity. Football and TV stars number among its summertime clientele. The esplanade (a favourite location for fashion shows) is replete with swimming pool and palm trees. Inside, a giant screen relays 24-hour cable TV broadcasts. By midnight, however, the DJ takes centre stage and the speakers positively shudder with sound. ⚘ *Areias de São João, Albufeira • Map G5 • 8pm–4am daily in summer*

5 Le Club Santa Eulália, Albufeira
A sophisticated nightclub with an eye-catching design and four different zones, including an á la carte restaurant. The main dance floor overlooks an oceanfront terrace. Dress up. ⚘ *Praia de Santa Eulália • Map G5 • (289) 598 070 • Midnight–6am Fri, Sat; restaurant: 8pm–midnight Tue–Sat*

6 Round Up Saloon, Carvoeiro

At the Round Up "outlaws" are locked up in a jail on the whim of Big Will the bartender and freed only on the promise of a beer. Live rock music is on most nights, and budding musicians are encouraged to jam. On Tuesday, Thursday and Saturday nights the karaoke cavalry arrives. ◈ *1 Estrada do Farol, Praia do Carvoeiro • Map E5 • 8pm–2am daily • Closed mid-Dec–mid-Apr*

7 Bowling Bridge Bar, Tavira

Under the Discoveries Bridge, half of this funky nightspot has a bowling alley where clubbers can strike out before hitting the dance floor. Known for its Latin music, "BBB" also hosts African-themed nights and popular DJ competitions. Upstairs is a chill-out lounge. ◈ *Estrada das Quatro Águas, Tavira • Map A5 • Daily: bowling 9pm–2am; bar 9pm–4am (6am Fri & Sat)*

8 Stevie Ray's Live Music Bar, Lagos

Toe-tapping live music on Friday and Saturday nights lifts this already excellent late-night bar to new heights. The atmosphere swings from jazz and blues to soul and house, when international DJs take to the stage. ◈ *9 Rua Srº da Graça, Lagos • Map D5 • 9pm–1am Tue–Sat • Adm on live nights*

Katedral, Praia da Rocha

9 Bar Amuras, Lagos

A popular lunchtime haunt, Amuras buzzes at night with a mix of funky DJ sounds and occasional live music. This is also a popular sports bar, broadcasting live events on big screens. ◈ *Marina del Lagos, Lagos • Map D5 • 10am–4am daily*

10 Katedral, Praia da Rocha

Bright red neon announces this temple of sound, dedicated to playing whatever's current. Its three bars flank a central dance floor that's never big enough to accommodate the throngs of party people. A sprawling terrace bar at the back affords great views of the beach and is an ideal chill-out spot. ◈ *Avenida Tomás Cabreira, Praia da Rocha, Portimão • Map E5 • 11pm–4am daily in summer*

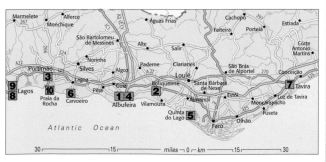

Left **Bifes de Atum** Right **Vineyard in the Algarve**

⁰¹⁰ Culinary Highlights of the Algarve

1 Ameijoas na Cataplana

If there is one dish synonymous with the Algarve's rich ocean harvest, it's this one. Fresh cockles are sealed in a *cataplana*, a rounded copper cooking vessel resembling a wok. Allowed to cook in their own steam with a combination of *presunto* (cured ham), *chouriço* (sausage), tomato, lemon, olive oil and garnished with coriander and garlic, the result is a succulent seafood delight. Enjoy with chilled white wine.

2 Arroz de Polvo

A regional speciality which again evokes the Algarve's love affair with the sea. Tender morsels of fresh octopus are added to a mix of fried onion and parsley, and then gently boiled with wine vinegar and a dash of chilli powder. Rice is added with salt and pepper to taste. The meal is usually served with a side dish of black olives and generous slices of crusty bread.

3 Sardinhas Assadas

The humble and ubiquitous sardine is arguably the most popular menu choice in the region. Bursting with goodness, sardines are at their plumpest

Porco à alentejana

Sardinhas assadas

Cabrito assado

during summer, and are simply mouth-watering when charcoal grilled and served with boiled potatoes and salad.

4 Bifes de Atum

The livelihoods of whole communities used to depend on tuna. It's not fished so hard now, but is still a favourite in thousands of restaurants along the coast. Try *atum de cebola*, a tasty blend of melted butter and tomato sauce with onions, garlic and parsley, poured over a firm tuna steak garnished with lemon wedges.

5 Cabrito Assado

Roasted kid is what country folk sit down to. The meat is brushed with a thin layer of lard to keep it moist, sprinkled with minced bacon and laced with white wine. Garnished with whole garlic cloves and dusted liberally with paprika, it's then slowly roasted until crispy brown. Rich and wholesome, this truly is one of the great gastronomic wonders of rural Algarve.

6 Porco à Alentejana

This intrepid marriage of pork and clams appears to bring the ocean and the countryside together, although it's a feast that originated in the vast plains of the Alentejo. The ingredients are cooked in a spicy marinade of white wine, fresh garlic and paprika. If prepared correctly, the shells should be open when served.

Doces de amêndoa

Frango Assado com Piri-piri

The great Portuguese stand-by: some restaurants in the Algarve serve nothing else. Generous platters of juicy chicken portions are served with crisp french fries and green-pepper salad. The meat comes dabbed with red chilli sauce, which is home-made and usually hot.

Gaspacho do Algarve

This version of gaspacho soup differs from its well-known Spanish counterpart in that the ingredients are not pulverized and so it retains a delightfully crunchy texture. Served cold, this heavenly blend of tomato, garlic, cucumber, oregano and sweet pepper sprinkled with diced crouton is bliss on a hot day.

Morgado de Figo

Figs were introduced by the Moors and soon became an integral part of Algarve cuisine. Fig lord cakes are dainty creations moulded from a fig-and-almond paste.

Doces de Amêndoa

Almonds (another Moorish import) are used to make these colourful little delicacies that can look like fish, fruit, birds, smiling faces and even vegetable baskets. They make wonderful coffee companions or little gifts.

Top 10 Algarve Wines, Liqueurs and Spirits

1 Vida Nova
Wine produced from Sir Cliff Richard's very own vines on his Algarve estate. With a rich, spicy bouquet, this red sings of young berry fruit.

2 Tapada da Torre
Flagship label from local winemaker João O'Neill Mendes. Both red and white are smooth on the palate.

3 Quê
A sparkling rosé made at the Barranco Longo vineyard from the *touriga nacional* grape.

4 Medronho
The celebrated *aguardiente* (brandy) is produced commercially, but the best is the "Monchique Moonshine", which is distilled in secret and sold with a nod and a wink.

5 Amarguinha
A sweet bitter-almond liqueur from the Algarve, ideal as an apéritif or digestif.

6 Barranco Longo
The Reserva Red is produced from *touriga nacional* and *syrah* grapes.

7 Aperitivo Algarseco
Underrated Algarvian dry white apéritif wine which is similar to an amontillado.

8 Licor de Tangerina
Wonderfully fragrant liqueur with the tang of lush citrus groves.

9 Brandy-mel
A potent mix of brandy and honey, this is a favourite mid-winter tipple.

10 Odelouca River Valley
Expressive, elegant and well balanced red wine from the Quinta do Francês winery. Connoisseurs take note.

For Alentejan wines See p108

Left **Quatro Águas, Tavira** Centre **Ocean, Alporchinhos** Right **Mirandus, Lagos**

⑩ Restaurants

1 Vila Joya, Albufeira

An exclusive gourmet restaurant boasting two Michelin stars. The menu degustation errs towards French haute cuisine, with a superb wine list to match. The terrace has a magnificent sea view. Tables are strictly by reservation only, and the dress code is on the casual side of smart. ◉ *Praia da Galé, Apartado 120, Albufeira • Map F5 • (289) 591 795 • www.vilajoya.com • €€€€€*

Chef, Vila Joya

2 Henrique Leis, Almancil

A Michelin star shines above this Swiss chalet-style restaurant where creativity and innovation are the hallmarks of the menu. Intimate surrounds are enhanced by colourful artwork. Smart to casual dress. ◉ *Vale Formoso, Almancil • Map J5 • (289) 393 438 • Closed Sun Jul–Aug, Sun & Mon Sep–Jun • No vegetarian dishes • €€€€€*

3 Adega Vilalisa, Mexilhoeira Grande

Renowned Portuguese food critic José Quitério regards this charming rural eatery as one of the

Henrique Leis, Almancil

best in the country. The tasting menu features dishes such as *canja de conquilhas* (cockle broth). Book in advance. ◉ *52 Rua Francisco Bivar, Mexilhoeira Grande • Map D4 • (282) 968 478 • Phone for opening hrs • No vegetarian dishes • €€€*

4 Casa Velha, Quinta do Lago

French haute cuisine is served in this 300-year-old converted farmhouse. It will appeal to the seasoned gourmet as well as the wine connoisseur, with over 200 Portuguese reds alone to choose from! ◉ *Quinta do Lago • Map J5 • (289) 394 983 • Visa and Amex only • Dinner only • Reservations required • Closed Sun & mid-Dec–Feb • €€€€€*

5 Quatro Águas, Tavira

A restaurant famed for its views over the lagoon as much for its wonderful *camarão vermelho flamejado* (flaming red shrimp) and *borrego com estragão* (lamb seasoned with tarragon). ◉ *Quatro Águas, Tavira • Map M4 • (281) 325 329 • Closed Wed & mid-Dec–Jan • €€*

6 Ocean, Alporchinhos

Executive chef Hans Neuner has won two Michelin stars at this intimate restaurant that uses local produce and has an international wine list. Wear elegant evening attire, and pre-book. ◉ *Vila Vita Parc, Rua Anneliese Pohl, Alporchinhos • Map F5 • (282) 310 100 • Vegetarian dishes on adv request • €€€€€*

Casa Velha, Quinta do Lago

Sueste, Ferragudo
The bizarre-looking but incredibly tasty *emparador* (emperor fish) is one of the more unusual treats on the menu at this fabulous quayside restaurant overlooking the River Arade. Spectacular summer sunsets bathe the terrace with a golden light, adding greatly to Sueste's appeal. ◎ *Rua da Ribeira 91, Ferragudo • Map E5 • (282) 461 592 • No credit cards • No vegetarian dishes • €€€*

Uniko, Vilamoura
The inventive cuisine at this restaurant on the marina surprises with its selection of home-made fare – the black cuttlefish risotto is a

Barbecued fish, Sueste

revelation. Sunday lunch choice includes British roast sirloin of beef with Yorkshire pudding, and treacle and beer glazed chicken breast. ◎ *Loja 21, CC de Marina de Vilamoura, Vilamoura • Map H5 • (289) 302 232 • €€€*

Mirandus, Lagos
This enchanting gourmet restaurant is perched on the top of a cliff with stunning views out to sea. You can choose from a five-course set menu, which changes every day, or make your selections à la carte. The wine list is an inspiration in itself. Book in advance. ◎ *Romantik Hotel Vivenda Miranda, Porto de Mós, Lagos • Map D5 • (282) 763 222 • €€€€€*

O Terraço, Martinhal
Traditional Portuguese cuisine is offered with flair and imagination at this contemporary restaurant. Serving hotel and resort guests, as well as non-residents, the emphasis is family-oriented, and the menu will appeal to both refined tastes and young palates. The wine list is impressive. ◎ *Hotel Martinhal, Martinhal • Map B6 • (282) 240 200 • Dinner only • €€€€*

AROUND THE ALGARVE

THE ALGARVE'S TOP 10

Left **Faro Marina** Centre **Carving, São Lourenço church, Almancil** Right **Church, Loulé**

Central Region

THE ALGARVE'S CENTRAL REGION *encompasses the busiest coastal resorts in southern Portugal as well as remote inland hamlets. It's an area of widely contrasting character, blessed with superb golf courses, beautiful golden beaches and wild, rolling hills where a more traditional, rural way of life prevails. History has left its indelible mark throughout this land in the shape of Stone Age megaliths, the remains of Roman villas, imposing Moorish castles and noble Gothic cathedrals. A strong, proud maritime heritage pervades the coast, evident in the fine selection of seafood in seaside restaurants.*

🔟 Sights

Bishop's Palace, Faro

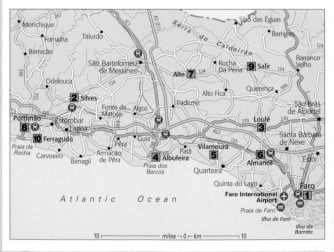

Previous pages **Quiet square in Tavira**

Faro

Faro is often overlooked by visitors to the Algarve who tend to head straight for the beach resorts. This is unfortunate, because its Old Town quarter is a particularly enchanting ensemble of centuries-old architecture and fine museums worthy of thorough investigation. Of special merit is the former convent of Nossa Senhora da Assunção, which houses the city's excellent archaeological museum *(see pp8 & 44)*.

Silves

Overlooking a fertile valley of lemon and orange groves, cork and almond trees and swathes of scented meadows is Silves. Once the grandiose capital of Moorish Algarve, the town's main draw is its castle. As well as taking the inspiring walk around its red sandstone battlements, visitors should look out for the fabulous vaulted Moorish cistern and Traitor's gate – the battle-scarred doorway through which Dom Paio Peres Correira stormed to recapture the stronghold for Christian forces in 1242. Outside the castle walls is the 13th-century cathedral, which was the seat of the Algarve see until 1580 *(see pp14–15)*.

Saturday market, Loulé

Loulé

This cheerful market town is renowned as a centre of traditional handicraft. The copper, leather and ceramic goods hammered out in the dozens of workshops dotted around its streets are some of the most sought-after in the Algarve. These can be purchased at Loulé's bustling Saturday morning market along with an amazing selection of fruit and vegetables, fresh fish, herbs, spices, honey, bottled liqueurs and sugared fig cakes. Loulé was an important Moorish settlement, and remnants of Muslim rule still exist *(see pp18–19)*.

Albufeira

Albufeira's claim as the most popular holiday destination in the country is no idle boast. It's the biggest and most energetic resort in the Algarve, and anyone doubting the fact should make a midsummer bee-line to the thoroughfare dubbed "The Strip". A forest of neon lends the resort its exotic, all-night atmosphere, and a multitude of bars, restaurants and disco-clubs keep the party swinging till dawn. You can catch up on sleep on any one of Albufeira's smooth, golden beaches, if you can find a spot amongst fellow sun-worshippers *(see pp30–31)*.

Silves

Left **Church, Almancil** Centre **Azulejos, Alte** Right **Praia de Rocha, Portimão**

5 Vilamoura

With its refined edge, glamorous reputation and celebrity status, Vilamoura is the resort choice for the well-heeled, where the yacht set and jet set rub shoulders. The boardwalk is also the jumping-off point for coastal cruises on graceful schooners, and shark and marlin fishing expeditions. The region as a whole is of great environmental and historical significance – the wetland surrounding the resort is a protected nature reserve, and the Cerro da Vila *(see p44)* is one of the most important Roman sites in Portugal. ◈ *Map H5*

6 Almancil

One of the most resplendent of all the Algarve's treasures is the 18th-century Igreja Matriz de São Lourenço, just outside the unexceptional town of Almancil. Outstanding *azulejos* panels in the church depict episodes in the life of St Lawrence, while the highly ornate cupola is a breathtaking exercise in trompe-l'oeil – some say the best example of its kind outside Rome. ◈ *Map J5*

7 Alte

Described as "a delightful snapshot of the real Algarve" in many a tourist brochure, Alte is indeed a picture of beauty and serenity. The little village with its whitewashed façades, filigree

---

The Carob Bean

The versatile carob bean tree is found in abundance throughout the Caldeirão mountain region. The beans are mainly used as animal feed but also as a chocolate substitute.
Pods can be ground and mixed with wheat flour to produce tasty black bread. The gum is used in the textile and pharmaceutical industries.

---

chimney pots and rural charm appears to have little time for the 21st century, but always greets visitors with a warm handshake and ready smile. The central attraction is the fonte picnic area near the stream. The area is also renowned for its handicrafts and colourful folklore. ◈ *Map H3*

8 Portimão

Portimão's attractive esplanade is lined with pretty gardens and a variety of quality restaurants and cafés. This is the departure point for river cruises along the Arade river; it's also the location of the first-class Museu de Portimão *(see p45)*. Autódromo Internacional do Algarve, a world-class racing track that has hosted the Le Mans Series and Superbike World Championships among other motorsports, is 8 km (5 miles) away. ◈ *Map E4*
• *www.autodromoalgarve.com*

Salir
9 In springtime, wild flowers of every hue blanket the meadows around this hilltop hamlet, with its ruined 12th-century Moorish castle. The terraced battlements are now reclaimed to ingenious effect by enterprising locals who use them as vegetable plots. The short walk around the castle foundations is rewarded with an inviting panorama over the limestone *massif* of Rocha da Pena. The area is a known nesting site for the huge eagle owl. Naturalists may also be lucky enough to spy the odd genet or Egyptian mongoose. ◈ *Map J3*

Ferragudo
10 Ferragudo has admirably managed to avoid the more garish trappings of tourism and looks the better for it. Sitting at the mouth of the Rio Arade, this attractive fishing village tumbles down to a busy little quayside bristling with fishermen's huts, artisan's workshops and one or two truly memorable seafood restaurants. The maze of steep cobbled alleys lead up to a rather handsome church. Praia Grande is a generous swathe of sand, which is popular sunbathing territory and also the location of a big windsurfing school. The beach is dominated by the monolithic Fortaleza de São João, a private residence. ◈ *Map E5*

Ferragudo

A Tour of Villages

Morning

An ideal starting point for your drive is **Loulé** *(p71)* on a Saturday morning to take advantage of the bustling market. An early start will ensure you get the best choice of the produce. Aim to get there about 9am and allow an hour for browsing the stalls.

Order a coffee in Café Calcinha, Praça da República, 67, before jumping in the car and heading west on the N270 to the village of **Paderne** *(p76)*. If you want to visit the 12th-century Moorish castle, turn right before the village.

To reach the next village, **Alte**, double back and head towards São Bartolomeu de Messines, turning right at the N124. Alte is now signposted, and about half an hour away. Lunch at one of the restaurants near the church.

Afternoon

Afterwards head for **Salir**, a leisurely, 25-minute drive away. Explore the castle ruins and admire the superb views of Rocha da Pena. If you have arrived on a weekday, the little museum will be open.

Continue east on the N124, driving through the Caldeirão mountain range before turning right onto the N396, back towards Loulé.

A signposted detour off this road will take you into the ancient hamlet of **Querença** *(p76),* with its whitewashed church and ancient stone cross. Take time to soak in the rural atmosphere, perhaps over a coffee, at one of the cafés overlooking the square.

Left **Carvoeiro** Centre **Querença** Right **Paderne**

Other Villages and Sights

1 Paderne
A world away from the villas and beaches of the Algarve coast. The faded, timeworn charm is mirrored by some lovely 19th-century buildings. The half dozen friendly café-restaurants dotted around the vicinity make for welcome refreshment. ◈ Map G4

2 Querença
A quaint hamlet slumbering in isolated beauty and crowned by the simple Igreja Nossa Senhora da Assunção. ◈ Map K4

3 São Bartolomeu de Messines
Poet João de Deus (1830–96) is synonymous with this quiet rural town. The church has some amazing twisted sandstone pillars – unique in the Algarve. ◈ Map G3

4 Barragem do Arade
Birdsong echoes around this huge, picturesque reservoir. A wonderful picnic spot, the rolling countryside is great hiking and mountain-biking territory. ◈ Map F3

5 Ameixial
Typical of the villages that pepper this rugged region. Nearby Miradoura de Caldeirão is an inspiring place for a picnic, and to the south are the last remaining examples of round dwellings. ◈ Map K2

6 Santa Catarina da Fonte do Bispo
The village is mainly famous for its traditional red clay bricks and roof tiles. Some of the local olive trees are believed to be more than 1,000 years old. ◈ Map L4

7 Estômbar
From this village follow the signs to Sítio das Fontes and discover a hideaway picnic spot overlooking the Arade river. An old water mill can be seen among the beautiful surroundings. ◈ Map E4

8 Praia do Carvoeiro
Picturesque beach wedged between steep-sided cliffs and framed by rows of holiday apartments and some excellent restaurants. A popular summer haunt for families and, during the winter months, golfers. ◈ Map E5

9 Alcantarilha
Known for its gruesome bone chapel, with the skeletal remains of 1,500 former parishioners completely covering the ceilings and walls. ◈ Map F4

The bone chapel at Alcantarilha

10 Alcalar
The Alcalar burial chambers are a series of Neolithic dolmen passage tombs. The drive here is a delight in itself, among ancient oak and olive trees. ◈ Map D4

Previous pages **Beach at Albufeira**

Left **Praia de São Rafael, Albufeira** Centre **Praia de Faro** Right **Praia da Marinha, Benagil**

🔟 Beaches

1 Praia dos Pescadores, Albufeira

The "Fishermen's Beach" is so called because of the dozens of colourful fishing smacks left on the sand between use. 🔍 *Map G5*

2 Praia de São Rafael, Albufeira

Some extraordinary rock formations protrude from the shallows of this pretty bay fringed with fine sand. 🔍 *Map G5*

3 Praia da Oura, Albufeira

Located at the bottom of "The Strip", this is a hugely popular beach in summer and attractive with its patches of yellow sandstone rock. 🔍 *Map G5*

4 Praia de Rocha, Portimão

One of the most famous beaches in the Algarve, this impressive swathe of golden sand stretches out in front of russet-coloured cliffs. 🔍 *Map E4*

5 Praia de Marinha, Benagil

An almost vertical cliff face towers over Marinha's two wonderfully secluded beaches, the waters of which are a favourite with snorkellers. 🔍 *Map F5*

6 Praia da Falésia, Olhos de Agua

A long, narrow beach that never gets too crowded in summer. It's

exposed to fresh south-westerlies so draws the windsurfing set. A good option if peace and quiet are the order of the day. 🔍 *Map H5*

7 Praia da Vilamoura

The beach at Vilamoura enjoys an enviable location right next to the resort. Its waters are calmed by the harbour breakwater, and the place is often used as a backdrop by fashion photographers. 🔍 *Map H5*

8 Praia do Vale do Lobo

This select beachfront is patronized by guests staying at the nearby Vale do Lobo resort and is always a hive of activity. There are some excellent barcafés close at hand. 🔍 *Map J5*

9 Praia de Faro (Ilha de Faro)

One of the narrow barrier islands that shelter the Ria Formosa lagoon, this giant sand spit is a magnet for Faro residents and those visitors wishing to escape the city heat mid-season.
🔍 *Map J–K6*

Albufeira

10 Praia da Galé, Armação de Pêra

Two half-moons of smooth white sand make up this beach, interrupted by some weird outcrops of ochre-splashed sandstone. 🔍 *Map F5*

Left **San Lorenzo Golf Course** Right **Balaia Golf**

Golf Courses

1 San Lorenzo
The magnificent, 18-hole, par 72 course is considered by *World Golf* magazine to be one of Europe's top five courses. ⑤ *Quinta do Lago • Map J5 • (289) 396 522*

2 Quinta do Lago South
Quinta do Lago South, a championship course, has hosted the Portuguese Open several times. It is especially notable for four excellent par 5 holes. ⑤ *Almancil • Map J5 • (289) 390 705*

3 Pine Cliffs
This 9-hole, par 33 clifftop course is set against a spectacular Atlantic Ocean backdrop. The last hole is named "Devil's Parlour". ⑤ *Praia da Falésia, Albufeira • Map G5 • (289) 500 113*

4 Vale do Lobo
The Royal Course incorporates the world-famous par 3 16th hole with an extensive carry over cliffs. The Ocean Course follows an undulating layout. ⑤ *Almancil • Map J5 • (289) 353 465*

5 Vilamoura Golf Courses
The Oceânico Old Course, Pinhal, Laguna, Millennium and Victoria courses are all fabulous 18-hole, par 72 layouts, in a beautiful setting with pinewood and lake. ⑤ *Vilamoura • Map H5 • (289) 310 333*

6 Oceânico Faldo and Oceânico O'Connor Jnr
The Amendoeira Golf Resort has two acclaimed 18-hole layouts – designed by golfers Sir Nick Faldo and Christy O'Connor Jnr. ⑤ *Amendoeira Golf Resort, EN529, Alcântarilha • Map F5 • (289) 310 333*

7 Vale da Pinta Course, Pestana Carvoeiro
An ancient olive tree spreads over one of the greens of the 18-hole Pinta course. The 18-hole Gramacho layout has some heavily bunkered greens. ⑤ *Pestana Golf & Resort, Carvoeiro • Map E5 • (282) 340 900*

8 Pinheiros Altos
An independent 27-hole, par 72 course built on the Quinta do Lago estate, embracing part of the Parque Natural da Ria Formosa. ⑤ *Q. do Lago • Map J5 • (289) 359 910*

9 Vilasol Golf
Known for its water hazards, this 27-hole, par 72 course is a suitable challenge for golfers of all handicap levels. ⑤ *Morgadinhos, Vilamoura • Map H5 • (289) 320 320*

10 Balaia Golf
Built on undulating terrain punctuated with umbrella pine, cork oak and carob trees, this executive 9-hole, par 27 course is at the Balaia Golf Village. ⑤ *Albufeira • Map G5 • (289) 570 442*

Pinheiros Altos Golf Club

 Around the Algarve – Central Region

Left **Loulé market** Centre **Porches Pottery** Right **Quarteira fish market**

Places to Shop

1 Loulé Market
One of the Algarve's biggest and most colourful markets, selling fruit and vegetables, fish, herbs, spices, honey, jams, cakes and local handicraft. ◊ *Praça da República, Loulé • Map J4 • 9am–2pm Sat*

Loulé market

2 Forum Algarve Shopping Centre
With an architectural design inspired by Faro's historical centre, this is the region's biggest shopping mall. ◊ *EN 125, Sítio das Figuras, Faro • Map K6*

3 Algarve Shopping Centre
Modern mall with national and international chains, hypermarket, multi-screen cinema and food hall. ◊ *EN 125, Guia • Map G4*

4 Quinta Shopping Mall
An elegant open-air mall with some designer boutiques beauty salons, sports outlets and several restaurants. ◊ *Quinta do Lago • Map J5*

5 Portimão Retail Park
Great for DIY enthusiasts, computer buffs and keen gardeners, and overlooked by a good café-restaurant. ◊ *Chão das Donas, EN 125 • Map E4 • 9am–10pm daily*

6 Apolónia Supermarket
The best supermarket in the land for imported foreign produce difficult to get elsewhere in Portugal. ◊ *Avenida 5 de Outubro, 271, Almancil • Map J5*

7 Porches Pottery
One of the first commercial ceramic outlets in the region. The vast array of glazed pottery and earthenware goods are all manufactured in-house. Superb value for money. ◊ *EN 125, Porches, Lagoa • Map F4*

8 Quinta do Morgado da Torre Vineyard
There are guided tours of the vineyard and a superb retail outlet. Splash out and buy a bottle of Tapada da Torre Reserva Viognier – one of the best wines in the Algarve *(see p65)*. ◊ *Penina, near Alvor • Map E4 • 10am–5pm Mon–Fri*

9 Quarteira Fish Market
The most famous market of its kind on the south coast; arrive early for the choicest fish and seafood. Superb value for money makes this popular with restaurateurs as well as the public. ◊ *Largo do Peixe, Quarteira • Map H5 • 9am–1pm Wed*

10 Garden Giga
A sprawling garden centre with a comprehensive display of shrubs, trees and cacti, plus jams, liqueurs, honeys and wine. ◊ *Guia, EN 125 • Map G4 • 8am–10pm daily*

Left **Kiss, Albufeira** Right **Katedral, Praia da Rocha**

TOP 10 Nightlife

1 Kiss, Albufeira
Possibly the best-known nightclub in Portugal. Attracting a mixed 20-something crowd, its resident and guest DJs spin a funky mix of house and hip-hop *(see p62)*.

2 Vilamoura Marina
A multitude of bars, eateries and late-night shopping. Spectacular firework displays round off many a long summer evening. ◈ *Map H5*

3 Vilamoura Casino
Sophisticated gaming room with baccarat, Portuguese dice, roulette (French and American), blackjack and 500 bigjackpot slot machines. The Mira Lago Room stages world-class music and dance. ◈ *Praça do Casino, Vilamoura • Map H5 • 7pm–3am daily*

Vilamoura Casino

4 Kadoc, Vilamoura
The biggest club in the Algarve draws thousands of revellers to its wild summer parties. Guests bump and grind on five tiered dance floors under a blaze of multicoloured light *(see p62)*.

5 Avenida Tomás Cabreira, Praia da Rocha
One of the first tourist resorts in the Algarve, with a long esplanade crammed with glitzy bars and trendy nightclubs. ◈ *Map E5*

6 Bahia Beach Bar-Restaurant
Already a popular beachfront restaurant, this is also a cool after-hours hangout, with live music on Sunday night. ◈ *Meia Praia, Lagos • Map D5 • 10am–1am daily (to 7pm in winter)*

7 Katedral, Praia da Rocha
A popular late-night dance venue with both young professionals and tuned-in youth. The music reflects current trends, with the base level way off the dial *(see p63)*.

8 Gecko Club, Vale do Lobo
With an Antoni Gaudí-style interior and an array of cocktails, this is a truly inspired option. ◈ *The Square (Praça) • Map J5 • Apr–Sep: 11am–3am • Closed Oct–Mar*

9 Melting Pot, Quinta do Lago
Jolly, English pub-style bar and restaurant heaving with jovial locals, seasoned expatriates and sunburnt tourists. ◈ *Lote 27 Quinta Shopping • Map J5 • 10am–2pm daily*

10 Le Club Santa Eulália, Albufeira
Cutting-edge interior design and a generous dance floor characterize this fashionable nightspot. ◈ *Praia de Santa Eulália, Albufeira • Map G5 • Midnight–6am Fri–Sat (from 10pm Jul–Aug)*

Price Categories

For a three-course meal for one with half a bottle of wine (or equivalent meal), taxes and extra charges.	**€** under €20
	€€ €20–€30
	€€€ €30–€40
	€€€€ €40–€50
	€€€€€ over €50

Left **Restaurante Evaristo, Albufeira** Right **O Barradas, Silves**

TOP 10 Restaurants

1 Ramires, Guia
Diners have been coming to this convivial restaurant since 1964 to sample the best chicken *piri-piri* in the Algarve. ⊗ *Rua 25 de Abril, Guia • Map G4 • (289) 561 232 • €*

2 A Ruína, Albufeira
The *pargo* (sea bream) and *robalo* (sea bass) are particularly good here. ⊗ *Cais Herculano (Praia dos Pescadores) • Map G5 • (289) 512 094 • Closed Jan–mid-Feb • €€€€*

3 Restaurante Evaristo, Albufeira
Chic beachfront eatery with great ocean views. Seafood and fish eaten al fresco doesn't get better than this. ⊗ *Praia do Evaristo • Map G5 • (289) 591 666 • Closed Dec • €€€*

4 Restaurante Veneza, near Paderne
This rustic-style eatery is famed for its hearty country fare and vast wine choice. ⊗ *Mem Moniz, near Paderne • Map G4 • (289) 367 129 • No vegetarian dishes • €€€*

5 Thai, Vilamoura
Gacng kiaw wan (green curry with chicken and coconut milk) is just one of the deliciously authentic meals served here. ⊗ *Avenida Marina, Vilamoura • Map H5 • (289) 302 370 • €€€*

6 O Barradas, Silves
Succulent meat dishes, fresh fish options, a

connoisseur's choice of wine and a charming rustic ambience all ensure a memorable dinner. ⊗ *Venda Nova, Palmeirinha • Map F4 • (282) 443 308 • Closed Wed • €€€*

7 Marisqueira Rui, Silves
Order *ameijoas na cataplana* (cockles in a *cataplana* pan) and you'll see why this is Algarve's most famous seafood restaurant. ⊗ *Rua Comendador Vilarinho, 32 • Map F4 • (282) 442 682 • Closed Tue • €€*

8 Sueste, Ferragudo
Renowned for its fabulous range of seafood dishes, such as *pargo* (red bream), grilled to perfection. The best tables are on the quayside; the interior has a magnificent domed ceiling *(see also p67)*. ⊗ *Rua da Ribeira 91 • Map E5 • (282) 461 592 • Closed Mon & Jan • €€*

9 O Charneco, Estômbar
A modest menu of succulent meat dishes draws a loyal clientele here. Culinary awards and caricatures of the proprietor adorn the walls. ⊗ *Rua D. Sancho II, 3 • Map E4 • (282) 431 113 • No credit cards • Closed Sun & Jan • €€*

10 A Quinta, Almancil
Lively menu, such as *assiete* of fish with Thai curry sauce. ⊗ *Rua Vale Formosa • Map J5 • (289) 393 357 • Dinner only; closed Sun; mid-Dec–Jan • €€*

A Ruina, Albufeira

Left **Castro Marim** Centre **Tavira** Right **Alcoutim**

Eastern Region

L ONG, NARROW SANDBANK ISLANDS *stretch along much of the coastline of the eastern Algarve (Sotavento). These natural barriers shelter a fragile lagoon ecosystem that is home to a staggering variety of flora and fauna. Tucked behind them are timeworn fishing villages and hamlets. Further east, beautiful Renaissance churches loom over picturesque towns and elegant cities replete with Roman bridges, Moorish castles and the distinctive pyramid-shaped rooflines. The sparse interior is Nature's preserve, underlined by a culture and heritage that's remained unchanged for centuries.*

Sights

1. Tavira
2. Parque Natural da Ria Formosa
3. Castro Marim
4. Reserva Natural do Sapal
5. Alcoutim
6. Estói
7. Cacela Velha
8. Olhão
9. Vila Real de Santo António
10. Santa Luzia

Moorish-style lattice door, Tavira

1 Tavira

Churches are emblematic of Tavira, with nearly 40 towers and spires piercing the town's skyline. Two are of great historical significance: the Igreja da Misericórdia, the Algarve's most important Renaissance monument; and the Igreja de Santa Maria do Castelo, final resting place of Dom Paio Peres Correia. The elegant Roman bridge spanning the River Gilão is another landmark that lends character to a town considered by many to be the most charming in the region *(see pp12–13)*.

2 Parque Natural da Ria Formosa

This vast realm of marshland, salinas and sand dune islands is home to the rare purple gallinule (a member of the coot family), among others. The lagoon habitat is one of the most important wetland zones in Europe. The park's headquarters are near Olhão. Three exciting nature trails, São Lourenço, Quinta do Lago and Olhão, provide excellent opportunities for observing wildlife at close quarters *(see pp24–7 & 50)*.

Reserva Natural do Sapal

3 Castro Marim

The timeworn frontier town of Castro Marim looms with genteel poise over the mouth of the River Guadiana, and its twin castles bear witness to the strategic importance the settlement played during centuries past. Grand views from the ramparts of the main 13th-century stronghold encompass the Reserva Natural do Sapal to the north and Vila Real de Santo António to the south. Spain shimmers in the distance *(see pp32–3)*.

4 Reserva Natural do Sapal

Much of this wetland park comprises working salt pans, but it's also a major winter feeding ground for spoonbill, greater flamingo, Kentish plover, avocet, black-winged stilt, Caspian tern and other birds. The visitor centre (closed Sat & Sun) is on the edge of the saltmarsh, and there's a lovely nature trail *(see p51)*.

Tavira

5 Alcoutim

The ramparts of a 14th-century castle still stand vigil over this delightful riverside hamlet nestling on the upper reaches of the River Guadiana. On the Spanish side, the slumbering village of Sanlúcar amounts to a mirror image of Alcoutim. Once upon a time these two neigbours were at war with each other and it was in the castle that Dom Fernando I of Portugal and his Spanish counterpart, Henrique II of Castile, signed a short-lived peace treaty in 1371. Boats regularly shuttle between the two villages. ⬦ *Map P1 • Castle 10am–1pm, 2–7pm (to 6pm in winter) daily • Adm*

6 Estói

The inland village of Estói basks in the glory of two major attractions: Pousada Palácio de Estói *(see p123)* and the Roman ruins at nearby Milreu. The renovated 19th-century palace retains its pink Rococo façade and period architecture. Twenty minutes' walk away, the well-preserved Roman ruins constitute a peristyle villa built in the 2nd century AD, weathered columns, baths decorated with fish mosaics and a temple. ⬦ *Map K5 • Milreu Roman Ruins Apr–Sep: 10:30am–1pm, 2–6:30pm Tue–Sun; Oct–Mar: 9:30am–1pm, 2–5pm Tue–Sun • Adm*

Cacela Velha

7 Cacela Velha

Thought to have been a Phoenician settlement in origin, this quaint coastal hamlet commands one of the most unspoilt locations in the Algarve. A patchwork of fields and meadows surround a bluff crowned by an 18th-century fortress. Lying in its shadow is the parish church, its whitewashed candescence playing off the façades of the fishermen's cottages lining the tiny square. ⬦ *Map N4*

8 Olhão

One of the liveliest fishing ports in the Algarve has some fine seafood restaurants to match. The whole town revolves around fishing, a fact exemplified by the 17th-century parish

Alcoutim

church, built with donations from the local fishermen. At the chapel of Nossa Senhora dos Aflitos, women pray for the safe return of their menfolk during bad weather. The style of the town's cube-shaped houses, with flat roof terraces and external staircases, reflects the close trade links once enjoyed with North Africa. ◈ Map L5

9 Vila Real de Santo António

The original settlement here was submerged by monstrous tidal surges in the early 17th century. It was re-born in the late 18th century when the Marquês de Pombal designed a new town based on the Lisbon grid system. The town now attracts Spanish day trippers from Ayamonte, just over the River Guadiana, which in turn is a magnet for sightseers from Portugal (see pp32–3).

Santa Luzia

10 Santa Luzia

Stunted palmeiras stud Santa Luzia's long esplanade, swaying lazily in the sea breezes. The village is synonymous with octopus, and dozens of empty covos (pots) can be seen stacked near the quay, the hapless contents of which are probably on the dinner table. Summer sea safaris depart from the quayside and cruise the waters off Ilha de Tavira. ◈ Map M5

A Drive to Alcoutim

Morning

🕙 A morning's drive north out of Castro Marim on the EN122 will take you through undulating hills, and lush valleys to the banks of the River Guadiana.

Allow a leisurely hour to get to **Alcoutim**. Ignore the IC27 highway; stay on the EN122 towards Junqueira and Azinhal. After 30 minutes you'll see a sign for Alcoutim on the right. Ignore this. Instead, carry on past the Barragem de Odeleite, a huge shimmering reservoir, and through several small hamlets. You'll reach a junction at Cruzamento. Turn right here towards Alcoutim.

🔖 Refresh yourself at any one of Alcoutim's cafés hugging the central Praça da República. Alternatively, **O Soeiro**, at the bottom of Rua Município, has an outside terrace near the quay.

Afternoon

After lunch, consider a mini-excursion to Spain. The local Portuguese barqueiro (boatman) will take passengers across the river to Sanlúcar, the mirror image of Alcoutim. An equally agreeable Spaniard will ferry you back when you're ready.

The alternative route back to Castro Marim, via the EN507 (follow signs for Vila Real), is one of the most inspiring in the Algarve. Call in at the little Museu do Rio in **Guerreiros do Rio** (p41), to find out about local life.

After Foz de Odeleite the road heads back to the hills before joining the EN122 and arrowing south.

Left **Praia de Manta Rota** Right **View of Ilha da Armona from Ria Formosa**

Islands and Beaches

1 Ilha de Tavira
A huge offshore sandbank stretching 11 km (6 miles) west from Tavira, connected to land by a ferry from Quatro Águas. Alternatively, a mini railway can get you there from the resort of Pedras d'el Rei. Map M5

2 Ilha da Armona
Popular with independent travellers, the beaches facing inland are served by bars and restaurants. A ferry from Olhão takes 15 minutes. Map L5–6

3 Ilha da Culatra
The beaches here enjoy splendid isolation, and nude sunbathing in the dunes is not uncommon. The ferry takes 45 minutes from Olhão. Map L6

4 Ilha de Fuseta
You can walk onto this island at low tide, while the waters of the lagoon provide a popular venue for windsurfers. Map M5

5 Praia do Farol
A beautiful sweep of sand on the bank of a long sandspit island. Farol can be reached by a 45-minute ferry ride from the Porta Nova wharf below Faro's Old Town district. There are also departures from Olhão.
Map L6

6 Ilha de Faro
This long sandy spit is reached by turning right off the main road just before Faro International Airport and walking across the causeway. It can get crowded in summer with Faro residents. Map K6

7 Praia do Ancão
A sublime beach opposite Quinta do Lago that narrows into a sand spit, the tip of which is the preserve of near-empty, tranquil dunes. Map J6

8 Ilha da Barreta
Boat departures from Faro's Porta Nova wharf shuttle visitors to this "deserted island", where wildlife can be observed. A bar-restaurant, O Estaminé, provides sustenance. Map K6

9 Praia de Cabanas
Less crowded than some of its neighbours, Cabanas' pristine beaches lie in peaceful seclusion and are reached by continuing westwards along the shores of Praia de Manta Rota. Map N4

10 Praia de Manta Rota
Part of a sweep of golden sand that arches from Vila Real de Santo António to the tip of Praia de Cabanas. Access is via Manta Rota and Alagoas. Map N4

Ilha de Faro

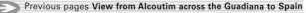

Around the Algarve – Eastern Region

Price Categories

For a three-course meal for one with half a bottle of wine (or equivalent meal), taxes and extra charges.	€ under €20
	€€ €20–€30
	€€€ €30–€40
	€€€€ €40–€50
	€€€€€ over €50

Left **Quatro Águas** Right **Faz Gostos, Faro**

🔟 Places to Eat

1 Quatro Águas, Tavira
Inspiring lagoon views. Try the grilled lamb dish *costeletas de borrego na grelha "a murro"*. 🕲 *Tavira • Map M4 • (281) 325 329 • Closed Mon & Dec–Jan • No vegetarian dishes • €€*

2 A Ver Tavira, Tavira
Trendy eatery next to the castle with tapas and a *menu de dégustation*. Booking essential. 🕲 *Calçada de Galeria, Tavira • Map M4 • (281) 381 363 • €€€*

Orangerie, Moncarapacho

3 Casa Velha, Cacela Velha
Set in a pretty hamlet, this quaint eatery attracts an enthusiastic clientele for its *feijoada de longueirão* (razor clams in bean stew) and other dishes. 🕲 *Cacela Velha • Map N4 • (281) 952 297 • Closed Mon • No vegetarian dishes • €*

4 Orangerie, Moncarapacho
Herbs from the garden and fresh seafood are used for dishes like octopus confit with codfish and *chouriço* purée. 🕲 *Sítio dos Caliços, Moncarapacho • Map L5 • (289) 790 790 • €€€€*

5 Marisqueira O Capelo, Santa Luzia
A table on the terrace with a view across the Ria Formosa is the best way to savour this classic fish and seafood restaurant. Specialities include tuna stew and octopus rice. 🕲 *Avenida Eng. Duarte Pacheco 40, Santa Luzia • Map M5 • (281) 381 670 • Closed Wed • No vegetarian dishes • €€*

6 A Tasca Medieval, Castro Marim
House speciality *açorda de galinha* (bread-based chicken stew) must be ordered in advance but is worth the wait. 🕲 *Rua 25 de Abril 65 • Map P3 • (281) 513 196 • Closed Tue • No vegetarian dishes • €*

7 Restaurante Ria Formosa, Olhão
One local describes this much-loved restaurant as "an ocean under one roof". The menu bursts with catches such as fresh *besugos* (mullet). 🕲 *Avenida 5 de Outubro, 14 • Map L5 • (289) 702 504 • Closed Thu • No vegetarian dishes • €*

8 Os Arcos, Vila Real
A large, cavernous seafood restaurant on the town's riverfront. 🕲 *Avenida da República, 45, Vila Real de Santo António • Map P4 • (281) 543 764 • No vegetarian dishes • €*

9 Luís dos Frangos, São Brás de Alportel
Down-to-earth place serving up succulent grilled chicken to an eager clientele. 🕲 *Rua Dr José Dias Sanchos 134, São Brás de Alportel • Map K4 • (289) 842 635 • Closed Mon and last 2 weeks Sep • No vegetarian dishes • €*

10 Faz Gostos, Faro

Dishes such as line-caught bass steamed with virgin olive oil are recommended, and Portugal's wines are well represented. 🕲 *Rua do Castelo 13, Faro • Map K6 • (289) 878 422 • Closed Sun • €€*

Left **Cabo de São Vicente** Centre **Vila Do Bispo** Right **Fishermen, Sagres**

Western Region

THE WESTERN ALGARVE *(Barlavento)* blends a precipitous Atlantic coastline with a verdant Mediterranean interior. The wild, windblown promontories associated with the legend of Henry the Navigator yield to forest-clad hills and cloud-tipped mountains. Some of the region's most spectacular beaches nestle on the south coast under outcrops of ochre-splashed rock. Others lie west to greet the surf that thunders onto the sand at the "end of the world". Underpinning the wonderful environmental fabric is a rich historical thread of Baroque churches and Manueline chapels, stark sea defences and baffling Neolithic monuments. Visitor attractions abound, with quaint restaurants in hushed villages waiting to be discovered, while lively resorts brushed by palm-lined avenues sway to a more cosmopolitan flavour.

Site of slave market, Lagos

🔟 Sights

1. Lagos
2. Monchique and Caldas de Monchique
3. Sagres
4. Cabo de São Vicente
5. Parque Natural do Sudoeste Alentejano e Costa Vicentina
6. Aljezur
7. Vila do Bispo
8. Raposeira Chapel
9. Barragém da Bravura
10. Odeceixe

Lagos

One of the most popular resort towns in southern Portugal, Lagos immediately captures the imagination with its carefree holiday spirit, laid-back lifestyle and immense historical wealth. Its greatest treasure is the Igreja de Santo António. The nearby

Ponte da Piedade, Lagos

beaches are equally attractive with their fine golden sand, ochre-splashed cliffs and bizarre outcrops of sandstone pillars (see pp20–23).

Monchique and Caldas de Monchique

Monchique, a rustic little market town, is tucked away in the forested Serra de Monchique under a mantle of towering eucalyptus and broad magnolia. Nestling in its shadow is Caldas de Monchique, a charming leafy hamlet glowing in the fame of its renowned spa facility where the sparkling mineral water is endowed with some remarkable curative properties. The Serra's unique Mediterranean-Atlantic habitat is a haven for wildlife. Sweeping views from Fóia and Picota crown this hugely diverse and fertile area (see pp16–17).

Sagres

Sagres's claim to fame is the huge landmark fort spread across the arm of the precipitous Ponta de Sagres. It's here that Henry the Navigator's original fortress and the Vila do Infante – his legendary school of navigation – is said to have been located. Little remains of either except for the giant pebble Rosa dos Ventos (wind compass) and the plain little chapel of Nossa Senhora da Graça, both supposedly used by Henry in the 15th century. Sagres itself is a modest town bestowed with a pretty harbour and some magnificent beaches that attract surfers from around the globe (see pp28–9).

Cabo de São Vicente

An austere landscape, dramatic limestone cliffs and a restless, unforgiving sea led Greek chroniclers to describe this windblown cape as the end of the earth. The Romans revered the rocky outcrop and called it Promontorium Sacrum, a place where the setting sun hissed in its dying embers as the ocean swallowed it up. The promontory retains an air of mystique. The cape's lighthouse is an important navigation reference point and looms over a former convent building. Henry the Navigator is said to have had a house in the small castle to the right of the tower. ◎ Map B5

Monchique

5 Parque Natural do Sudoeste Alentejano e Costa Vicentina

The entire coastline of western Algarve lies within the boundaries of this wild and rocky nature reserve. Dozens of scarce and endemic plant species thrive here – it's a botanist's paradise. Hundreds of different species of birdlife flutter and glide above the salt marshes, while, not surprisingly, ornithologists gather with binoculars primed.

Park headquarters, Rua Serpa Pinto 32, Odemira, Alentejo • (283) 322 735

6 Aljezur

The humble ruins of a 10th-century Moorish castle stand sentinel-like over a higgledy-piggeldy collection of whitewashed houses and café-restaurants that constitute the village of Aljezur. A steep, cobbled path leads up to the timeworn but sturdy castle walls and the splendid view beyond. This riverine area was once a breeding ground for malaria-carrying mosquitoes, and in the 18th century some of the villagers were persuaded to relocate to Igreja Nova, Aljezur's "modern" counterpart to the east. *Map C3*

7 Vila do Bispo

The landscape around Vila do Bispo is rich with evidence of the Algarve's prehistoric past. Mysterious *menhirs*, also known as megaliths, dot the countryside. Near Hortas do Tabual, a number of these stones, some bearing crudely carved crosses, appear to form a circle. Archaeologists speculate this could be the site of the mythical Church of the Raven, supposedly where the remains of St Vincent were interred before being taken to Lisbon.

Menhir circuit, Hortas do Tabual, Vila do Bispo • Map B5

Vila do Bispo

8 Guadalupe, near Raposeira

Considered to be one of the oldest examples of Gothic architecture in the Algarve, the unassuming 14th-century chapel near the town is of great significance. Henry the Navigator was said to have prayed here when he lived in the nearby town of Raposeira, as did many a crew before departing for unknown lands. Inside the chapel, built in honour of the Virgin of Guadalupe, enigmatic stone heads peer down from the ceiling.

EN 125, Raposeira • Map B5 • May–Sep: 10:30am–1pm, 2–6:30pm; Oct–Apr: 9:30am–1pm, 2–5pm • Closed Mon • Adm

Aljezur

Barragém da Bravura

9 Barragém da Bravura

The huge, man-made lake 10 km (6 miles) north of Lagos is a wonderful place to unpack the picnic hamper. In spring, fields of orchids nestle under delicate umbrellas of almond blossom, with butterflies flitting from bloom to bloom. Towering eucalyptus encroach upon the lakeside, and the woods are a favourite haunt of red foxes and wild boar. The higher ground north of the dam is generously wooded with cork oak, and it's from this area that the best views of the lake can be enjoyed. ◈ Map D4

10 Odeceixe

The River Seixe meanders past this pretty little village, which makes a handy base for surfers keen to ride the big swells that thunder onto Odeceixe beach. A lone windmill sitting above the village used to take advantage of the fresh winds whipped up by the Atlantic in days gone by; today it's a popular spot as a vantage point for scanning the Alentejo countryside. The good value guesthouses found here quickly fill up during the summer. This sleepy backwater is about as far as you can get from the summer throngs that pack the coastal resorts. ◈ Map C1 • Windmill Jun–Sep: 9am–noon, 2–6pm Tue–Sat

A Tour of the West

Morning

Breakfast in **Lagos** *(see p91)* can be enjoyed at the café in Praça Infante Dom Henrique near the castle walls, before you set out to explore the west coast.

The drive follows the EN125, crossing the boundary of the **Parque Natural do Sudoueste Alentejano e Costa Vicentina**. The road winds on – via the tiny 14th-century chapel of Nossa Senhora da Guadalupe and the prehistoric sights of **Vila do Bispo** – to **Sagres** *(p91)* and its landmark 17th-century fort.

For an invigorating walk and to further appreciate the seascape at Sagres, follow the path around the promontory.

By now, it should be time for refreshments at Café-Restaurante Cochina on Praça da República or, for something more substantial, the Café-Restaurant Pau de Pita on Rua Comandante Matoso.

Afternoon

Sagres has a pretty harbour which can be investigated on foot. Perched on a bluff overlooking the fishing boats are the ruins of Fortaleza da Baleeira which can be reached by turning up onto the dirt track off the roundabout near the quay.

No trip to the west coast would be complete without a visit to **Cabo de São Vicente** *(p91)* which is a short drive northwest. The clifftop vistas are truly awe-inspiring and a suitably dramatic way to end the day's sightseeing.

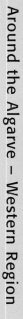

Left **Praia do Armado, Carrapateira** Centre **Meia Praia, Lagos** Right **Praia de Odeiceixe**

🔟 Beaches

Praia de Dona Ana, Lagos
A spectacular and intimate picture-postcard beach, framed by extraordinary outcrops of ochre sandstone. A warren of caves and grottoes runs through the base of the nearby cliff face. ◈ *Map D5*

Praia do Armado, Carrapateira
One of the surfer's favourites, Armado's Atlantic swells attract enthusiasts keen to ride the surf back into the wide sweeping beach. ◈ *Map B4*

Praia de Odeceixe
The River Seixe runs into this delightfully secluded stretch of sand, tucked away right up in the northern reaches of the Algarve, close to the Alentejo border. ◈ *Map C1*

Praia de Figueira, Salema
This popular beach fronts the tidy fishing village of Salema and attracts a young, sporty crowd, with windsurfing running a close second to sunbathing. ◈ *Map C5*

Meia Praia, Lagos
At 4 km (2 miles), this is one of the longest beaches in the Algarve, with plenty of room for sunbathers to share the sand with water-skiers and windsurfers. ◈ *Map D5*

Praia de Dona Ana, Lagos

Praia de Burgau
One of the best locations in the area for snorkelling and diving, the beach skirts Burgau resort and is hemmed in on either side by sloping cliffs. ◈ *Map C5*

Praia do Martinhal
Another fabulous location for windsurfing, with the ocean lapping a golden swathe of sand. The beach is also conveniently situated near the town of Sagres. ◈ *Map B6*

Praia do Beliche
The steep climb down a cliff path to the beach is rewarded with a wonderfully secluded wedge of pristine sand that sees few visitors because of its somewhat awkward location. ◈ *Map B5*

Praia da Luz
A fine beach with very easy access to resort amenities, Luz can get crowded mid-season. But there's always some room, especially towards its eastern flank. ◈ *Map C5*

Praia de Monte Clérigo
Another preferred beach of the surfing set and tourists possessed of a more independent spirit. An isolated landscape with untamed breakers. ◈ *Map C2*

Previous pages **Terraced farmland, Monchique**

Left **Canoes at Martinhal** Centre **Surfboarder** Right **Coastal walkers**

🔟 Outdoor Pursuits

1 Horse Riding
With its almond and cork oak trees, the area around Bensafrim, northwest of Lagos, is idyllic riding territory. ✪ *Quinta do Paraiso Alto riding centre, Fronteira • Map C4 • (282) 687 596 • www.qpahorseriding.com*

2 Diving
Some of the best dive sites off the Iberian peninsular are found along the Algarve's south-western coast. Subterranean chasms and shallow reefs are easily reached. ✪ *Map D5 • www.blue-ocean-divers.de*

3 Bird Watching
The Cabo de São Vicente headland offers a superb vantage from which to observe birds in spring and autumn, when the skies are dotted with eagles, storks, falcons, finches and an astonishing variety of gulls. ✪ *Map B5*

4 Surfing
The Atlantic rollers pummelling Praia do Armado lure many surfers. Competitions take place throughout summer. ✪ *Map B4 • www.algarvesurfcamp.com*

5 Mountain Biking
The western Algarve's myriad patchwork of coastal and inland trails, tracks and paths make for some excellent mountain bike circuits for all levels. ✪ *Map D5 • www.the mountainbikeadventure.com*

6 Coastal and Inland Walks
A favourite is the footpath from Luz to Burgau. It starts in open countryside, follows the coastline along the lip of a cliff, then slopes to the sea. ✪ *Map C5 • www.portugalwalks.com*

7 Big Game Fishing
Warm coastal waters (Jun–Sep) attract marlin and sharks. Sports fishermen usually return triumphant from the "fighting chair". ✪ *Pescamar, Lagos Marina • Map D5 • (966) 193 431 • www.pescamar.info*

8 Canoeing
The calm waters of the Alvor estuary are perfect for canoeists, with opportunities to stop on sandy beaches. ✪ *Map D4 • (282) 969 520 • www.outdoor-tours.com*

9 Ancient Archaeology Tour
Dating back at least 5,000 years, *menhirs* stud the area around the village of Vila do Bispo (see p92). ✪ *Menhir circuit, Hortas do Tabual, Vila do Bispo • Map B5*

10 Kite Surfing
One minute you are surfing, the next you are airborne. The best season for this exhilarating watersport is May–Oct, but wind conditions are good all year round. Sheltered lagoons are ideal places for beginners. ✪ *Map E5–L6 • www. kitesurfeolis.com*

Archaeological tour

Left **Lagos Surf Centre** Right **Aljezur Gypsy Market**

Places to Shop

1 Rua Cândido dos Reis/ Rua 25 de Abril, Lagos

The busiest streets in town, where shoppers can browse the rows of stores and boutiques for jewellery, handicrafts and fashion. ❧ Map D5

2 Casa dos Arcos

One of the few places in the Algarve where you can purchase *cadeiras de tesoura*, the folding wooden chairs, which are hand-crafted to an ancient Roman design. ❧ José Salvador, Estrada Velha, Monchique • Map E3

Casa dos Arcos

3 Mediconforto

Handy health food shop with a huge selection of minerals, vitamins, homeopathic remedies and natural cosmetics. ❧ Rua Soeiro da Costa 26, Lagos • Map D5

4 Atelier Opalina

A stunning range of hand-made jewellery fashioned out of gold, silver, mother-of-pearl and precious stones. ❧ Praça do Infante, 1, Lagos • Map D5

5 Lagos Surf Center

An outlet for O'Neill, Ripcurl, Billabong and Quicksilver, you'll find everything you need to surf here, including a dizzying choice of boards and pretty beachwear. The guys behind the counter can arrange surf schools and safaris, as well as other watersports. ❧ Rua Silva Lopes 31, Lagos • Map D5

6 Baptista Supermarket

Baptista is known for its fresh regional produce. On Saturdays at 11am there are live cooking demonstrations, with tasting sessions later. ❧ Montes da Luz, Praia da Luz • Map C5

7 Sagres Natura Surfshop

Come here for the wide range of top-brand surfwear, boards and accessories. They also run a well-established surf school and rent kayaks and mountain bikes. ❧ Rua de São Vicente, Sagres • Map B6

8 Aljezur Gypsy Market

A lively gypsy troupe trundles into Aljezur on the third Monday of every month with an extraordinary array of clothing, household items and foodstuffs at bargain prices. ❧ Map C3

9 Mercado da Avenida

A bustling fish market with a rooftop terrace restaurant and splendid views across the harbour. ❧ Avenida dos Descobrimentos, Lagos • Map D5 • 8am–2pm Mon–Sat

10 Intermarché

On the main approach road to Sagres, this is the place to stock up on food, drink, toiletries and everyday essentials. Clothes, shoes, tools and kitchenware are also on sale. There's an on site café, too. ❧ ER268, Sagres • Map B6

Price Categories

For a three-course meal for one with half a bottle of wine (or equivalent meal), taxes and extra charges.

€	under €20
€€	€20–€30
€€€	€30–€40
€€€€	€40–€50
€€€€€	over €50

Left **As Dunas, near Sagres** Right **Mullens**

Places to Eat

1 Adega Vilalisa, Mexilhoeira Grande

A rural gem with fine traditional cuisine, including succulent pork knee roast *(see also p66)*. ◈ *52 Rua Francisco Bivar, Mexilhoeira Grande • Map D4 • (282) 968 478 • Dinner only • No credit cards • No vegetarian dishes • €€€*

2 No Pátio, Lagos

A charming restaurant popular with foodies *(see also p67)*. ◈ *Rua Lançarote de Freitas 46, Lagos • Map D5 • (282) 763 777 • Tue–Sat dinner & Sun lunch • €€€*

3 Mullens, Lagos

Full of character and run by friendly staff. The Mozambique-style beef is incredible. ◈ *Rua Cândido Reis, 86, Lagos • Map D5 • (918) 480 071 • Dinner only, closed mid-Jan–Feb • €*

4 Adega Papagaio, Espiche

Choose from seven different meats, all chargrilled on a hot stone. ◈ *Rua da Adega, Espiche, nr Lagos • Map C5 • (282) 789 423 • Dinner only • €*

5 Cabrita, Carrapateira

The owner is equally proud of his fresh fish and an autograph by late Beatle George Harrison on a one-dollar bill. ◈ *8670-230 Bordeira Carrapateira • Map B4 • (282) 973 128 • No vegetarian dishes • Closed Wed • €€*

6 As Dunas, near Sagres

This stylish kid-friendly beachfront venue serves up a healthy range of fresh fish and tasty seafood. ◈ *Quinta da Martinhal, near Sagres • Map B6 • (282) 240 200 • No disabled access • €€€*

7 Bica Boa, Monchique

Opt for the terrace during fine weather for a wholesome al fresco treat in idyllic surrounds. ◈ *Estrada de Lisboa, 266, Monchique • Map E3 • (282) 912 271 • €*

8 Vila Velha, Sagres

Oven-baked stuffed quail with muscatel wine and raisin sauce is just one of the eclectic dishes here. ◈ *Rua Patrão António Faustino, Sagres • Map B6 • (282) 624 788 • Tue–Sun dinner; closed Jan & Feb • €€€*

9 A Eira do Mel

This rural Slow Food member offers a superb Atlantic wild shrimp *cataplana*. ◈ *Estrada do Castelejo, Vila do Bispo • Map B5 • (282) 639 016 • Closed Sun & Mon lunch • €€*

10 Cacto, Odiaxere

Creamy pepper, garlic or blue cheese sauce tops the tournedos "fillet" steak at this lively eatery. ◈ *EN 125, Odiaxere • Map D4 • (282) 798 285 • Closed Wed & Thu • €€*

Adega Vilalisa

Left **Lusitano horse** Centre **Monsaraz rooftops** Right **Granite figures in Évora**

The Alentejo

UNDULATING PLAINS *and blistering summer heat characterize much of this province to the north of the Algarve. Blankets of yellow wheat sway across huge tracts of land, and much of the sun-baked earth is pocked by stubby cork and olive trees. Vines trace emerald lines across ochre soil to surround whitewashed villages. To the north, medieval settlements perch on steep, granite escarpments in an altogether rockier terrain. While, down by the coast, secluded beaches of golden sand brush sleepy, unhurried resorts that wake up in summer, when the days are long and the air is warm.*

TOP 10 Sights of the Alentejo

1. Évora
2. Marvão
3. Mértola
4. Monsaraz
5. Castelo de Vide
6. Vila Viçosa
7. Beja
8. Estremoz
9. Elvas
10. Serpa

Share your travel recommendations on traveldk.com

Praça do Giraldo in Évora

museum. Crowning all this is a castle commanding dramatic views of the Serra de Marvão and the borderlands. ⊗ Tourist info: Rua de Baixa • (245) 909 131

1 Évora

The historic centre of Évora, capital of the Alentejo, is listed as a UNESCO World Heritage Site. Stunning examples of Roman, Moorish, medieval and 17th-century architecture abound in the narrow streets and breezy squares. The central Praça do Giraldo has a wonderful 16th-century fountain. A walk from the square up the lively Rua 5 de Outubro leads to the grandiose Sé (cathedral). An adjacent 16th-century palace houses the Museu de Évora. The nearby Roman temple is the best preserved monument of its kind in Portugal. *(See the itinerary on p103.)* ⊗ Tourist info: Praça do Giralde 73 • (266) 777 071

2 Marvão

Named "the eagle's nest" by locals, this medieval hamlet, set high upon on a rugged escarpment, is an astonishing sight. Sinuous 13th-century battlements envelope an immaculate village, where polished cobbled streets snake past neat façades, white-washed cottages, a dainty church, trim gardens and a cherished

3 Mértola

Designated a *vila museu*, or open-air museum-town, the old quarter of Mértola is divided into a number of areas of historic interest. Each reflects the diverse periods in the town's history: Phoenicians, Romans, Visigoths and Moors all took advantage of its strategic position on the River Guadiana. A number of museums exhibit treasures from each period, but the most stunning collection can be found in the Museu Islâmico. ⊗ Tourist info: Rua de Igreja 31 • (286) 610 109

4 Monsaraz

Swathes of vineyards surround Monsaraz, a name synonymous with some of the finest Portuguese wine. The views from the granite walls of the 13th-century castle take in the huge man-made lake that has transformed the countryside *(see p106)*. At dawn the rising sun paints the water's surface a blaze of orange. The village's Igreja Matriz holds court over a maze of lanes lined with squat dwellings and tucked-away restaurants. ⊗ Tourist info: Rua Direita • (927) 997 316

Left **View from Marvão's castle** Right **Mértola**

→ For more information on the area, go to www.visitalentejo.pt

Left **Castelo de Vide** Right **Paço Ducal, Vila Viçosa**

Castelo de Vide

The old Jewish quarter is the most enjoyable part of this attractive hill-top town. It stretches away from the 13th-century castle that gives the town its name in a cluster of steep lanes, many sporting plaques testifying to the quality of their floral displays. A synagogue (also 13th-century) sits at the top of this stepped thoroughfare, which also leads down to the 16th-century marble Fonte da Vila. ⍟ *Tourist info: Praça Dom Pedro V • (245) 908 227*

Vila Viçosa

During the 15th century Vila Viçosa became the country seat of the dukes of Bragança and the town is best known today for its splendid Paço Ducal. The semi-ruined battlements of the dukes' former abode, the castle, surround a collection of brightly painted cottages and the 14th-century church of Nossa Senhora da

Conceição. ⍟ *Tourist info: Praça da República • (268) 889 317*

Beja

A thriving agricultural town and capital of the Baixo Alentejo, Beja also has a rich past displayed in museum buildings that are often as interesting as their exhibits. The Convento de Nossa Senhora da Conceição, for example, now houses the Museu Regional, and the town's oldest church, the 6th-century Santo Amaro, is home to the Museu Visigótico. The landmark Torre de Menagem (castle keep) dates from the late 13th century.
⍟ *Tourist info: Rua Capitão João Francisco de Sousa 25 • (284) 311 913*

Estremoz

Dominating this graceful town is the Torre das Três Coroas, the Tower of the Three Crowns, named in honour of kings Sancho II, Afonso III and Dinis. You can gain free access to the tower via the adjoining castle and palace. The nearby Museu Municipal is housed in a 17th-century almshouse. Among the exhibits are some wonderful examples of *bonecos*, pottery figurines typical of

Chapter house, Beja's Museu Regional

Aqueduct between Amoreira and Elvas

the region. ✆ *Tourist info: Rossio Marquês de Pombal • (268) 339 227*

9 Elvas

Chunky pentagonal bastions, thick walls and gaping moats surround this busy frontier town near the Spanish border. The 17th-century fortifications resemble a multifaceted star and are very well preserved – they are best viewed from the castle. Within the walls are the excellent Museu Municipal and Biblioteca and the tiny 16th-century church of Nossa Senhora dos Aflitos. The mighty Aqueduto da Amoreira stretches between Elvas and a spring some 5 miles (8 km) away at Amoreira. ✆ *Tourist info:* ✆ *Tourist info: Praça da República • (268) 622 236*

10 Serpa

This tranquil town makes for leisurely exploration. Start with the city walls and the stout towers of the Porta de Beja. Up above are the remains of an 11th-century aqueduct. Within the walls the castle provides the strongest focal point, and its ramparts offer sweeping views of the Alentejan plains. Finally, leave time to sample some *queijo de Serpa*, a creamy ewe's milk cheese often served as a starter. ✆ *Tourist info: Rua Dos Cavalos 19 • (284) 544 727*

A Day in Évora

Morning

🕐 Begin at the **Praça do Giraldo** and wander up Rua 5 de Outubro towards the **Sé (cathedral)**. Look out for the 14th-century carved Apostles flanking the portal and, once inside, climb to the treasury to see the 13th-century ivory figure of the Virgin.

Adjacent to the cathedral is the **Museu de Évora**, where a dazzling 16th-century Flemish polyptych, *Life of the Virgin*, can be found upstairs.

On the opposite side of the square are the granite Corinthian columns of the **Templo Romano** – the best-preserved Roman monument in Portugal.

🔗 From here, retrace your steps back to Praça do Giraldo for lunch or a coffee at **Café Cozinha de Santo Humberto**.

Afternoon

📍 Take Rua da República, on the eastern side of Praça do Giraldo. A few minutes' walk brings you to Praça 1 de Maio lorded over by the huge 16th-century Manueline-Gothic **Igreja de São Francisco**.

The church's principal draw is the **Capela dos Ossos (Chapel of Bones)**. The skeletal remains of some 5,000 monks line the walls and columns of the chapel. An inscription above the entrance reads, *"Nós ossos que aqui estamos, pelos vossos esperamos"* ("We bones that are here await yours").

📍 Time to rest, maybe back at one of the cafés on Praça do Giraldo.

 Following pages **Bull fight, Monsaraz castle**

Left **Serra do São Mamede** Centre **Cromlech of Almendres** Right **Monastery, Crato**

Best of the Rest

1 Viana do Alentejo
A little backwater famed for its natural springs, but also home to a fine 14th-century castle and a fortified church. Peacocks roam round the pilgrim church of Nossa Senhora de Aires, 20 minutes' walk east of the town centre.

2 Serra de São Mamede
This beautiful and diverse nature reserve is home to a stunning variety of wildlife: Bonelli's eagle, Egyptian vulture, genet and the Iberian midwife toad are some of the residents.

3 Cromlech of Almendres (Guadalupe)
The Cromlech of Almendres stone circles are considered the most important megalith group in the Iberian peninsula. Nearby is the Neolithic Dolmen of Zambujeiro.

4 Vila Nova de Milfontes
An attractive seaside resort hugging the River Mira near a vast swathe of golden sand. Popular in summer, with superb surf.

5 Portalegre
The superb Museu do Guy Fino (named in honour of the founder of Portalegre's last remaining tapestry factory) showcases some of the finest examples of tapestry in Europe.

Folk crucifix, Portalegre

6 Évoramonte
Dramatic views reward those who make it to Évoramonte's castle walls which are embellished with curious stone "ropes". Dom Miguel ceded the throne in Évoramonte on 26 May 1834.

7 Arraiolos/Pavia
The foundations of the castle at Arraiolos date back to Celtic times, while in Pavia, 18 km (11 miles) to the north, a tiny chapel has been built into a dolmen – architecturally unique in Portugal.

8 Crato
Neat rows of whitewashed houses with yellow trim characterize this town, once the headquarters of the 14th-century Order of Hospitallers. Exhibits in the Museu Municipal explain more about Crato's illustrious past.

9 Redondo
Dozens of hole-in-the-wall *olarias* (pottery workshops) line the narrow streets of Redondo, which makes it a worthy stop-off to pick up a slew of ceramic souvenirs.

10 Barragem de Alqueva
The Alqueva dam project led to Europe's biggest artificial lake. A lakeside marina at Amieira runs houseboat sightseeing holidays, and there is a fine restaurant serving traditional cuisine.

Left **Rua 5 de Outubro, Évora** Right **Locally grown vegatables, Alentejo**

Places to Shop

1 Rua 5 de Outubro, Évora

Lined with *artesanatos* (handicrafts shops) bristling with ceramics, carved cork, copper *cataplanas* (cooking pots), hand-painted chairs, occasional tables and other curios. On the second Tuesday of every month a lively open-air market takes place across the Rossio de São Brás, just outside the town walls.

2 Rua de Cima 7, Marvão

An incongruous but very useful minimarket, squeezed in between rows of stone cottages, caters to residents and self-catering travellers alike. There are also one or two *artesanatos* in the same street.

3 Divinus Gourmet, Évora

Mouthwatering selection of over 500 gourmet goodies, including chocolates, jams, patés and wines. ◈ *Mercado Municipal de Évora, Praça 1 de Maio, Évora*

4 Coisas de Monsaraz

Home-made jams and other assorted knick-knacks can be bought from this friendly little arts and craft shop nestling in the shadows of the castle walls. ◈ *Largo do Castelo 2, Monsaraz*

5 Charcutaria, Castelo de Vide

Bottles of wine, honey, sweets and cakes, and spicy sausages make up some of the regional goodies for sale in this traditional *loja* (shop). ◈ *Rua de Olivença, 29*

6 Mercado Municipal, Vila Viçosa

Housed is a modern complex in the town centre, the market is at its busiest early on Saturday mornings when it overflows with fresh fruit and vegetables, and a wide selection of fish. ◈ *Largo D. João IV • 9am–1pm, daily*

7 Rua Afonso Costa, Beja

A narrow, atmospheric precinct lined with fashion boutiques, traditional handicrafts shops and cafés.

8 Antiquidades, Estremoz

Beautiful and original antiques fill this small shop near the Torre das Três Coroas in the old quarter. The Saturday market (in the lower town, across the Rossio) is the place to buy goat's and ewe's milk cheeses and the famous preserved plums.

9 Rua de Alcamim, Elvas

A busy pedestrianized street with florists, music stores, shoe shops and the usual handicrafts. The weekly Monday market takes place near the impressive Aqueduto da Amoreira.

10 Sabores da Terra, Serpa

The wooden counter and decorated tiled floor of this former grocery store lend it an authentic feel. This is one of the best places to buy the rich and creamy Serpa cheese, as well as other traditional Portuguese products. ◈ *Praça da República*

Left **Selection of wines** Right **The wine-producing region of Vidigueira**

Top Ten Alentejan Wines

1 Marquês de Borba Reserva (Tinto)

Robust red from the João Portugal Ramos stable. Blended from Periquita, Aragonês and Trincadeira grape varieties and matured in French oak, this deep crimson delight enhances casseroles and roasts.

2 Esporão Garrafeira (Tinto)

Complex wine showing ripe fruit and well-integrated oak characters with rich, textured tannins, superb balance and long, flavoursome aftertaste. A perfect match with hearty, Alentejan fare.

3 Quinta do Mouro (Tinto)

Harmonious blend of ripe fruit flavours with a jolly 14 per cent alcohol content. Deep crimson with rich, oak finish and full-bodied bouquet. Enjoy with game.

4 Herdade Grande Colheita Selecionada Branco (Branco)

A delicious wine with ripe, aromatic peach and melon fruits. Rich, full palate with creamy texture and soft finish. Wonderful with baked fish, salad or chicken.

5 Esporão Touriga Nacional (Tinto)

Has typical violet and dark berry fruit aromas with toasty oak complexity. Palate is firm with rich spicy fruit characters. Complements pastas and red meat.

6 Dolium Regional Alentejano Branco (Branco)

Made exclusively from the Alentejo's top white grape variety, Antão Vaz, to produce a wine of citrus colour with fragrant toast and vanilla spice aromas. Superb with fish dishes.

7 Cortes de Cima (Tinto)

Dark and concentrated in colour with a ripe, red-berry-and-cherry aroma enhanced by subtle hints of spicy French and American oak. Excellent with steak and game.

8 Vila Santa (Tinto)

A deep violet wine made from Trincadeira, Aragonês, Cabernet Sauvignon and Alicante Bouschet grape varieties. Smooth on the palate and a healthy companion with *javoli* (wild boar).

9 Outeiro (Branco)

Soft white that shows a spicy aroma of tropical fruits. Made from the Roupeiro, Arinto and Antão Vaz grape varieties. Ideal chilled as an aperitif.

10 D'Avillez (Tinto)

This esteemed red is produced here by Jorge d'Avillez and is smooth, soft and rounded. Perfect with roasted pork.

Price Categories

For a three-course meal for one with half a bottle of wine (or equivalent meal), taxes and extra charges.

€	under €20
€€	€20–€30
€€€	€30–€40
€€€€	€40–€50
€€€€€	over €50

Left **Fialho** Right **Cabrito assado** (roast kid), a favourite dish of rural Portugal

🔟 Places to Eat

1 Fialho
Local specialities at this popular restaurant include *cacão de coentrada* (dog fish served with coriander sauce). Advance booking is essential. ✍ *Travessa dos Mascarenhas 16, Évora • (266) 703 079 • Closed Mon • €€*

2 São Rosas
Superb location right in front of the Torre das Três Coroas, matched by first-class service. Top puddings. ✍ *Largo D. Dinis 11, Estremoz • (268) 333 345 • Closed Mon • €€€€*

3 Restaurante Casa do Povo
Sweeping terrace views in one of Portugal's most beautiful mountain villages makes dining here a real treat. The *bifes de vitela* (veal steaks) are highly recommended. ✍ *Travessa do Chabouco, Marvão • (245) 993 160 • Closed Thu • €*

4 Restaurante D. Dinis
This country-style eatery serves a regional menu based around succulent grilled meats. A limited wine list includes some fine Alentejo reds. ✍ *Rua D. Dinis 11, Beja • (284) 325 937 • Closed Wed & 1–15 Aug • No vegetarian dishes • €*

5 Xarez
A select menu of authentic regional fare is served at this chic, traditionally styled restaurant/bar with breathtaking views and sunsets. Monsaraz and Reguengos wines feature prominently. ✍ *Rua de Santiago 33, Monsaraz • (266) 557 052 • No vegetarian dishes • €*

6 Tombalobos
The modern fine-dining take on much-loved Alentejo recipes here has earned nationwide praise. The *petiscos* (bite-size appetizers) are delicious, and the generous wine cellar will impress. ✍ *Avenida Movimento das Forças Armadas, Portelegre • (245) 331 214 • Vegetarian dishes on request • €€*

7 Os Cucos
Set in verdant, shady gardens, with a daily-changing menu erring towards earthy Alentejan fare. An outside terrace has coffee and snacks. ✍ *Mata Municipal, Vila Viçosa • (268) 980 806 • €*

8 Restaurante Panorâmico da Amieira
Try to get a terrace table at this restaurant perched over a beautiful lake. Delicious Alentejo fare is served, and the soups are a revelation. ✍ *Amieira Marina, Amieira • (266) 611 175 • Times vary; call ahead • €€€*

9 Restaurante Alentejano
Order the *ensopado de borrego a pastora* (lamb stew shepherdess' style) for a real taste of the Alentejo. ✍ *Praça da República, Serpa • (284) 544 335 • Closed Sun pm, Mon • €*

10 Pousada Vila Viçosa – D. João IV
Opt for the regional menu at this beautiful venue for inspired Alentejo cooking. Dishes are based on nuns' recipes with a twist. ✍ *Convento das Chagas – Terreiro do Paço, Vila Viçosa • (268) 980 742 • €€€*

STREETSMART

THE ALGARVE'S TOP 10

Left **Road sign** Centre **Faro airport** Right **Ferry, Vila Real de Santo António**

🔟 Getting to the Algarve

1 Visa and Entry Requirements

You will need a valid passport to enter Portugal, but no visa is required for EU nationals. Those arriving from Canada, New Zealand or the USA can stay for a maximum of 90 days in any half-year without a visa.

2 By Air From Within Europe

The entry/exit point for visitors by plane is Faro International Airport. The national airline, TAP Air Portugal, operates daily scheduled services between Faro and Lisbon and Oporto. SATA connects Faro with Lisbon, Madeira and the Azores. Low cost airlines, such as easyJet and Ryanair operate summer charter flights from around Europe to Faro. There are connections with many international flights out of Lisbon.

3 By Air From the Rest of the World

Faro International Airport serves both domestic and foreign carriers, all of which arrive and depart from the same terminal. In high season the airport gets very busy, and delays can be expected.

4 Faro Airport

The airport is 6 km (4 miles) outside the city. Several Eva buses depart from outside the arrivals hall, starting at 5am and running to 11:15pm (9:15pm weekends).

The information desk has detailed timetables. There are taxis here too. All the major international car hire companies have offices at the airport.

5 By Road From Lisbon

A tolled motorway (A2) links the Portuguese capital, Lisbon, with the Algarve. Ordinarily, this journey will take around three hours, but in summer queues can form at the toll booths. An alternative route is the toll-free IC1, which runs parallel to the IP1 and IP2.

6 By Road from Spain

The Ayamonte-Huelva toll-free motorway links the Algarve with the Spanish towns of Seville, Córdoba and Madrid.

7 By Scenic Coastal and/or Hill Route

An alternative way to drive to the Algarve from Lisbon is to follow the IC1 to Mimosa, then turn onto the N263 towards Odemira. Go through this town to the N120 which follows the boundaries of the Parque Natural do Sudoeste Alentejano e Costa Vicentina. This wonderfully scenic route eventually takes you to Lagos but adds at least another hour onto your journey. Alternatively, come off the N263 before Odemira and follow the N266 to Monchique – a long but very pretty drive.

8 By Bus/Coach

There are excellent express coach services to Faro from towns and cities right across Portugal. The two main coach companies are EVA Transportes SA and Renex. It is best to pre-book tickets from the main bus stations.

9 Aerodromes

The Algarve is served by two aerodromes at Alvor, near Portimão, and Lagos. Private jets and light airplanes also fly in and out of Faro International Airport. Alvor and Lagos aerodromes operate rentals as well.

10 Boat

On the south coast, the well-equipped, large marinas at Lagos, Vilamoura, Albufeira and Portimão (Praia da Rocha) all serve the international yachting community. A smaller marina is located at Vila Real de Santo António. A daily passenger ferry connects this eastern Algarve border town with Ayamonte in Spain.

Directory

Flight Information
(289) 800 800 • Faro Airport • Map K6 • www.ana.pt

Alvor Aerodrome
Near Portimão • (282) 495 828

Lagos Aerodrome
(282) 762 906

Left **Taxis** Centre **Regional train** Right **Cyclists, Praia do Armado**

🔟 Getting Around the Algarve

Roads and Tolls
The road system in the Algarve is generally very good, though some back roads are no more than dirt tracks. The A22 motorway (Via do Infante) is electronically tolled. Portuguese licence plates are read by radar. A fee based on distance travelled and class of vehicle is payable within five business days. See www.visitportugal.com for more details; car rental offices can also provide information.

Rules of the Road
Driving is on the right. The speed limit through towns and villages is 50 km/h (35 mph), 90 km/h (60 mph) on A-roads outside built-up areas and 120 km/h (80 mph) on the motorway. Safety belts (front and back) are compulsory, and children under 12 are not allowed to ride in the front. Drivers must also carry a red warning triangle in case of accident or breakdown.

Car Rental
All the major car hire companies have offices in the main towns, but Faro International Airport is the usual pick-up/drop-off point. To hire a car (over 21s only), you'll need a passport and a full international driving licence.

Coach Services
The Algarve is well served by coach and bus companies, with daily connections between a network of coastal and inland towns. Tickets must be pre-booked and can be purchased from main bus stations. Express services have WCs on board and some provide video entertainment.

Local Bus Services
Cost effective, if slow, local bus services operate well between most coastal towns. Always put your arm out to flag down an approaching bus, and note that bus stop signs (*paragem*) can be on the opposite side of the road.

Rail Services
CP (Caminhos de Ferro Portuguese) operate a regional train service (no reservation necessary) along the Algarve coast between Vila Real de Santo António and Lagos, with several trains daily in each direction. You have to connect at Tunes for inter-regional and Alfa Pendular trains heading north (which must be pre-booked).

Taxi Services
Taxis use a fixed tariff system, so establish the price before setting off. The minimum flat rate is €5, a telephone booking adds €2, and luggage in the boot adds €3. Rates jump up 20 per cent 10pm–6am, on weekends and public holidays. Tipping, around 10 per cent of the total fare, is at your discretion.

Helicopters
Almancil-based HTA Helicopters Lda operate a fleet of modern, comfortable helicopters with a maximum range of 700 km (500 miles). They can be hired for business or leisure (such as aerial photography).

Boats and Yachts
The River Guadiana is navigable from Vila Real de Santo António up to Alcoutim, and it's also possible to sail partly along the Arade, though this stretch is really the preserve of sightseeing tour boats. Coastal excursions are popular, and there are several marinas for safely docking yachts.

Cycling
In Portugal, cycling is more sport than leisure, which unfortunately means there are few cycle paths. Mountain biking is more popular, and the Algarve hills have some great treks.

Directory

Eva Coaches
Faro • (289) 899 700
• www.eva-bus.com

Renex Coaches
Faro • (289) 812 980

Train Information
(808) 208 208
• www.cp.pt

HTA Helicopters Lda
(289) 435 112

Left **Tourist brochures** Centre **Newspaper stall** Right **City signs**

General Information

Algarve Regional Tourist Board

The ERTA head office can supply the addresses and telephone numbers for all regional tourist offices. Their website (www.visit algarve.pt) is in English and Portuguese and is regularly updated with news and visitor information.

Internet Sites

Three merit particular mention for their ease of use, the useful information supplied and the links they offer. Browse them at: www.portugal-info.net, www.visitportugal.com, www.algarveuncovered. com and www. inspirationsalgarve.com.

Classifieds

123 Algarve is a weekly newspaper published in English, German and Portuguese featuring hundreds of classifieds, from property to services, and an entertainments supplement.

ERTA Pamphlets

Algarve Guide is a free monthly pamphlet published on behalf of the ERTA. It's a goldmine for information on museums, markets and cultural events, and it is available at most tourist offices. Listings are in English and Portuguese.

Tourist Magazines and Newspapers

Essential Algarve is a glossy, bi-monthly publication featuring useful articles on spa resorts, golf courses, property, travel and finance. It is published in English and Portuguese. *Welcome to the Algarve* is a free English-language monthly newspaper with restaurant reviews, sightseeing tips and useful pull-out city maps. Find it in restaurants, bars and shops.

Local Newspapers and Books

An Algarve institution, *The Resident* is a weekly English-language publication packed full of news, views and comments. *The News* is a national, weekly, English-language newspaper that includes Algarve domestic news. Books on the Algarve written by locals include *Southern Portugal: Its People, Traditions and Wildlife*, which delves into the history and culture of almost every town and village in the southern Alentejo and Algarve.

Weather

Spring and autumn are the best times to visit. The winter months are mild – temperatures rarely fall below freezing. July and August can be uncomfortably hot.

Opening Hours at Sights

Major museums are usually open 10am–5pm Tuesday to Sunday. Some close for a two-hour lunch break. Major churches are open during the day without a fixed timetable, although some may close between noon and 4pm. Smaller churches may only be open for services.

Public Holidays

The following days are public (bank) holidays in Portugal: 1 January; Carnival Tuesday in February/March (variable), Good Friday, March/April (variable); Revolution Day, 25 April; May Day, 1 May; Portugal Day, 10 June; Feast of the Assumption, 15 August; Immaculate Conception, 8 December; Christmas Day, 25 December.

Municipal Holidays

In addition to the above, every town celebrates a local (municipal) holiday, affecting opening times and sometimes public transport schedules. Check with the local tourist office.

Directory

ERTA Head Office
Avenida 5 de Outubro, 18, Faro • (289) 800 400/424

Tourist Information Free Helpline
In English and several other European languages • (289) 800 400 (9am–6pm Mon–Fri)

Left **Museum, closed on Mondays** Centre **Fresh fish, not on Mondays** Right **Sign for campsite**

🔟 Things to Avoid

1 August in the Algarve

It's not easy to find accommodation unless booked well in advance, and bars, restaurants and clubs are uncomfortably full. Instead, consider visiting in the early part of September.

2 Swimming When a Red Flag is Up

A red flag hoisted over a beach indicates that the water is unsafe, either because of a strong tide or powerful undertow, and swimming is prohibited. A yellow flag means that paddling at the water's edge is allowed. When a green flag is flying the water is safe. Note that a black and white chequered flag means the beach is temporarily unsupervised. A blue flag means the beach has been noted for its excellent water quality and environmental sustainability.

3 Drinking and Driving

The maximum legal blood-alcohol level in Portugal is 0.05g per litre (two small beers or a glass of wine). Be sensible and do not expect any leniency. Those caught can expect a night in the cells (probably a whole weekend if you're pulled over on a Friday), a swift court appearance, a heavy fine and possibly even a jail sentence.

4 Discarding a Lit Cigarette

The entire Algarve is tinder-dry mid-summer and very susceptible to forest fires. Under no account light open fires away from designated barbecue areas; never discard a lit cigarette or match in the countryside. A dedicated toll-free number (117) should be used to report a wildfire.

5 Signing a Time-Share Deal

Refuse point-blank to sign up to any timeshare scheme on the street. If you are interested in purchasing real estate in this manner the best advice you can seek is from someone who has successfully – and happily – already done so and make a note of the property agent involved.

6 Speeding

Drivers caught speeding in Portugal are subject to an instant, on-the-spot fine. You'll also be asked to produce an identity card or passport, driving licence, insurance certificate and vehicle log book, and proof of ownership. Better to ease up on the pedal.

7 Visiting Museums on Mondays

Many museums are closed on Mondays. There are some exceptions, but it's always better to check ahead rather than arrive and be disappointed.

The same goes for public holidays, although during the summer these official days off are often ignored in favour of extra business.

8 Conducting Business between 1pm and 3pm

Lunches are long. The Latin notion that it takes two hours to savour a dish of sardines and half a bottle of wine rings true throughout much of the region, especially in rural areas, and particularly on Fridays.

9 Buying Fish on Mondays

Many trawler crews take Sunday night off and only resume work the following evening. This means that fish for sale on Monday mornings might have been caught some 12 hours earlier and refrigerated before ending up in the market.

10 Camping on Beaches

This is strictly a no-go. The Portuguese character is very welcoming and accommodating, but the authorities do not take kindly to flagrant disregard of its countrywide policy banning camping on its beaches, particularly along the west coast where there are large expanses of deserted beach. Regular police patrols ensure that miscreants receive a substantial fine if discovered.

Left **Pottery shop** Centre **Fish market** Right **Loulé shopping street**

🔟 Shopping Tips

Visit a Market at the Busiest Time
To get a real flavour of the Algarve's markets, go in the early morning when they are at their busiest. This is when the locals are out bagging the best deals. The fish market at Quarteira (daily, except Sunday) and Loulé's fantastic Saturday market are most vibrant at 9am.

Shop Hours
Normal shop hours are 9am–1pm and 3pm–7pm, Mon–Fri. In rural areas most shops close Saturday afternoons and all day Sunday. In the tourist zones, however, many proprietors extend their opening hours throughout the evening.

Malls and Hypermarkets
It's easy to spend several hours in one of the modern shopping malls, such as Forum Algarve (Faro), Algarve Shopping (Guia) and Aqua Portimão. There, large international stores and hypermarkets sell everything under the sun and usually stay open till 10pm. They are also open on Sundays (some shops within the malls do shut). Cinemas, children's play centres, bars and restaurants are all on hand.

Budget Day
If shopping within a budget, steer clear of imported brands, no matter how much they remind you of home. Tinned goods especially are vastly overpriced. In any case, the Portuguese equivalent is generally equal in quality and certainly better value.

Taxes – Lighten the Load
There's no more duty-free shopping in Portugal's airports, but non-EU tourists should look out for the Europe Tax-Free Shopping Portugal logo displayed in shops. In some circumstances non-EU citizens are eligible for an IVA (Imposto Sobre Valor Acrescentado), or sales tax refund. Minimum purchase is around €59. The goods, refund cheque and your passport should be presented at Faro customs on departure for a refund by post.

Shellfish Shopping
The Algarve is famed for its *marisco* (shellfish), and the choice is bewildering. Open-air markets and supermarkets have shellfish counters where stock is packed in ice or submerged in water to keep it fresh and moist. The best time to shop for seafood, though, is really during the colder months when it's at its tastiest.

Finding the Best Pottery
Ceramic and earthenware goods are typical of the Algarve's more traditional wares and make great souvenirs. The small village of Porches, just off the EN125 between Alcantarilha and Lagoa is famed throughout Portugal for its ceramics. Porches Pottery has an outstanding array of cups, mugs, plates, saucers, pots and vases for sale.

Roadside Bargains
The Algarve has splendid citrus fruits, especially oranges. Some of the biggest, sweetest and juiciest can be bought from the simple roadside stalls scattered around inland towns and villages, especially near Silves.

Catch a Cataplana
The *cataplana* is one of the Algarve's most characteristic copperware goods. It is used for cooking stews and is shaped like a wok, with a snap-down concave lid. The best can be bought in Loulé, in artisan shops near the market.

Monchique Moonshine
If you're after the best *medronho (aguardiente – brandy)*, head for Monchique and seek out the homemade moonshine. This local firewater is made from the berries of the *arbutus*, or strawberry tree. Those in the know say that the best has a yellow tinge to the otherwise clear liquid.

Left **Restaurant menu board** Centre **Café, Lagos** Right **Local liqueur**

🔟 Eating and Drinking Tips

1 Believe Word of Mouth Recommendations

Despite the glossiest of brochures and the slickest of advertising, nothing sells a restaurant menu better than word of mouth. It's the best recommendation you can have, especially if it's from someone you know. Some restaurants trumpet their menu choice without taking too much care about the ingredients. Take time to ask around rather than settling for the nearest. The listings within this guide are the author's recommendations.

2 Order Sardines in Summer

When it comes to sardines, they are best eaten during the summer months. This is when they are firm and at their plumpest. The fish must be charcoal-grilled the same day they are caught to ensure optimum flavour.

3 Consider the Dish of the Day

For a quick, inexpensive meal, simply order the *prato do dia* (dish of the day) from the menu, whatever it happens to be. Locals often ask for the *prato do dia*, and it often proves to be the best choice – invariably wholesome, probably cheaper than the rest of the menu, and served up with little delay.

4 Ask for Half Measures

If you're not too hungry but would still prefer a meal to a snack, ask for a *meia dose* or *mini-prato* (half portion). Most restaurants are happy to oblige. This is also a good option for children.

5 Specify Your Beers

When you ask for *cerveja* (beer) you'll get a lager. To order draft beer, ask for *uma imperial* (small beer) or *uma caneca* (large). If you prefer a bottle, order *uma garrafa de cerveja*. The two top brands are Super Bock and Sagres; both also brew *cerveja preta*, the nearest you'll get to a brown ale.

6 Tip the Right Amount

Tipping depends on how much you enjoyed the food and the quality of service. Between 10 per cent and 15 per cent of the total bill is usual.

7 Watch Out for those Extras

The sliced bread, glistening olives and tuna fish paste that land on your table before the meal begins in earnest is listed as *couvert* on the menu. You should decline the offer and send them back if you don't want them. Then check that they haven't been included in the final bill, which occasionally happens as an honest mistake.

8 Look at the Wine Label

The choicest wines are those with the description *reserva a garrafeira* on the label. Expect to pay more for these wines and those of vintage quality.

9 Smoking

Portugal introduced a ban on smoking in public places in 2008 and though not as wide ranging as elsewhere in Europe, the rules are rigorously enforced. Small bars and restaurants can opt to allow smoking (indicated by a blue *fumadores* sign) provided they have adequate ventilation. Otherwise look out for red *não-fumadores* signs. The law is less flexible elsewhere, including shopping centres.

10 Use the Complaints Book if Necessary

All restaurants have, or should have, a *livro de reclamações* (complaints book). Don't be put off using it if you have a genuine grievance and keep a copy of the entry. If eating in a hotel restaurant the complaints procedure is relatively straightforward. Elsewhere, you may have a harder job, especially in some rural areas. That said, service is generally very good everywhere and there'll be few instances when you have to seek redress.

It's not easy being vegetarian in Portugal; whenever possible, phone a restaurant first to check if they will prepare a vegetarian meal.

Left **Public phone booth** Centre **Post boxes** Right **Post office**

🔟 Banking and Communications

1 Banking Hours
Banking hours are 8:30am–3pm Monday to Friday. Monday mornings tend to be busy, so if you have bank business to attend to get there early.

2 Changing Money
Look for the desks marked *câmbios* to change travellers' cheques. Banks charge up to €12.50 commission, exchange bureaux about €5. Travellers' cheques can also be changed at some hotels, but check the charges first, as they vary considerably.

3 Money Through the Wall
A far easier way to obtain funds is via an automatic teller machine (ATM). Visa, AmEx, Access/Mastercard or similar can be used to withdraw cash in euros, and most machines have instructions in several languages. Look for the blue *multibanco* sign.

4 Using Credit Cards
Major credit cards are widely accepted in the main towns, but always ask if in doubt and make sure your brand of card is accepted. In rural areas, however, it's best to carry cash.

5 Post Offices
Post offices open weekdays 8:30am–6pm. The branch in Faro, on Largo do Carmo, is also open on Saturday mornings. There are two services: *Correiro normal* and *Correiro azul*. The former is for ordinary post and airmail, and red post boxes should be used for such mail. *Correiro azul* is the priority/express service and uses blue post boxes.

6 Telephone Cards
Telephone cards *(cartão telefónico)* are available from post offices, shops and newsagents. The only drawback is the difficulty ascertaining how many units you have left.

7 Mobile Phones
The Vodafone office in Faro International Airport can advise visitors on their mobile phone *(telemóvel)* options. For example, if your mobile is not locked to a specific network, you can purchase a SIM card that can be topped up with credit and will connect your phone to one of the local networks.

8 Directory Enquiries
Dial 118 and the operator will ask you in Portuguese what number you require. Though most operators speak English, ask your hotel for assistance if you don't speak Portuguese.

9 Tuning In
The Algarve has its very own English-language radio station. Tune into Kiss FM (95.8 and 101.2FM) for news and flight bulletins, weather reports, commercials and some pretty good music.

10 Internet and Email Access
The quickest and easiest way of staying in touch with home is often via email. Boxed here are ten of the best Internet cafés in the Algarve.

Internet Cafés

Caves d'el Rei Snackbar, Tavira
Rua Dr Carlos Palma, 18A

Bora Café, Lagos
Rua Conselheiro Joaquim Machado, 17

Club 39 Bar, Armação de Pêra
Rua Dr José António dos Santos

Netpoint, Loulé
Rua José Fernandes Guerreiro, 28

Casa dos Condes, Alcoutim
Praça da República

Pastelaria Traquino, Ferragudo
Rua Marechal Carmona, 27A

RB C@fé, Rocha Brava
Loja F, Urbaniz Rocha Brava-Alfanzina

Café Bilhares, Faro
Largo de São Pedro, 9

Left **Pharmacy sign** Centre **Sun-lovers** Right **Hospital sign**

10 Security and Health Matters

1 Calling Emergency Services

To contact the emergency services dial 112 (toll-free). Most operators speak at least two foreign languages, usually including English.

2 Hospitals in the Algarve

There are three main hospitals in the region: Faro district hospital, Portimão and Lagos. All towns have a *centro de saúde* (health centre) that can deal with less serious medical problems.

3 Medical Insurance

Citizens of the EU are entitled to free emergency or reduced cost treatment if they possess an EHIC (European Health Insurance Card), or equivalent, and a valid passport. Visitors from elsewhere should ensure they have adequate health insurance for emergency medical care and extra cover if, for example, surfing, diving or horse riding.

4 Pharmacies

In Portugal, *farmácias* (pharmacies) are easily identified by their green cross sign. These are found everywhere in larger towns but are not so abundant in rural communities. Usually very well supplied, many have English-speaking staff and sometimes German, Spanish and French speakers in the

resorts. There's always a pharmacy open late; look for the list of late-night services posted on pharmacy windows.

5 Safety on the Beach

Safety flags fly over the beaches throughout the summer and should not be ignored. A green flag means it's safe to swim; a yellow one means only paddling is allowed; red indicates that it's unsafe to enter the sea.

6 Avoid Sunburn

With near cloudless skies, there's a very real risk of serious sunburn, so be sure to use a sunscreen lotion that's strong enough for your skin type. The sun is fiercest between noon and 3pm, when it's best to seek out a parasol or shady beachfront café.

7 Don't Dehydrate

Drink plenty of water! Tap water is safe. There's also a vast choice of bottled mineral water – *com gaz* (fizzy) and *naturale* (still). In midsummer, aim to drink around two litres a day.

8 Precautions Against Theft

Petty theft is increasingly common in the Algarve, so take a few sensible precautions, such as not flaunting expensive watches and cameras, and never leaving

valuables unattended. Avoid leaving personal items in the car, even in the boot – hire cars are easily recognized by would-be thieves.

9 Identification

Always carry some means of identification with you and have car documents to hand when driving. Failure to produce identification if stopped by the police may result in a hefty fine, even if you are blameless in all other respects.

10 Loss of Passport

Report such a loss to the police immediately. You should also inform your embassy or consulate. To facilitate enquiries, make copies of all important documents and leave them in your room safe or another secure place.

Directory of Hospitals

Faro District Hospital
Rua Leão Penedo
• *(289) 891 100*

Portimão (Barlavento) Hospital
Sítio do Poço Secu
• *(282) 450 300*

Lagos Hospital
Rua Castelo dos Governadores
• *(282) 770 100*

Left **Camping, Albufeira** Right **Public transport**

Top 10 Ways to Save Money

1 Visit in Low Season

For some spectacular bargains, visit in January and February. Although many places are closed for the winter, prices for accommodation can be as much as 50 per cent less than in peak season. Alternatively, during the summer, consider an all-inclusive package.

2 Take a Tent

This is the cheapest option in the Algarve, but you must use official campsites. There are dozens along the coast and quite a few inland. Prices do rise during the high season, but you can still expect to pay only around €10 per adult per night for a small tent.

3 Stay in Youth Hostels

If you're eligible, staying in youth hostels is another inexpensive option, although there are no single room rates and prices can creep up in the summer. There are six hostels in the Algarve at: Alcoutim, Faro, Portimão, Lagos, Tavira and Aljezur. If you don't already have a Hostelling International card from your national hostel association you can obtain a "guest card". Advance booking is essential in summer.

4 Rent a Quarto

Local tourist offices can sometimes provide a list of homeowners renting out *quartos* (private rooms), with shared facilities, at very reasonable rates. It is also possible to rent the occasional beach hut on a strictly temporary basis. Again, the tourist office may be able to help. Otherwise look out for *quarto* signs in windows, on notice boards etc.

5 Get a Youth Discount Card

Popular youth-card schemes such as Euro<26 and Go25/IYTC allow card holders good discounts on a wide range of attractions and services, including travel, museum and cinema tickets.

6 Get Discounted Rail Travel

For discounts on Alfa Pendular and Intercity train services it is worth looking online up to 30 days in advance of when you want to travel. There are offers for senior citizens, children, Youth Card holders and 2-for-1 offers. You can also purchase tickets in advance at mainline stations. These discounts do not apply to regional services.

7 Eat with Locals

Whenever possible, eat where the locals eat. It may be no more than a 'hole-in-the-wall' taverna, and the fare may be presented without finesse, but the food will be much cheaper than opting for a beachfront restaurant. The *prato do dia* (dish of the day) is usually the cheapest on the menu.

8 Use Public Transport Instead of Hitch-hiking

While hitch-hiking may cost next to nothing, it's not recommended in Portugal. The Portuguese have an ambivalent attitude towards hitch-hikers. You may catch a lift within minutes or you may stay all day on the same spot. It's much easier to use the cheap and efficient public transport. A sobering reason not to try and hitch-hike is the appalling road safety record held by Portuguese drivers.

9 Drink Sensibly and in "Happy Hour"

It's worth noting "Happy Hour" times posted outside bars in resorts. Discounts can be substantial, though the hours when prices are lowered often entice you to drink earlier in the day. Enjoy the savings but behave responsibly.

10 Buy the Cheapest Cinema Tickets

On Mondays, cinemas across Portugal offer discounted seats, but be prepared to queue, especially if you want to see the latest Hollywood blockbuster. Foreign films are never dubbed but subtitled instead.

Left **Balaia Golf** Centre **Two-pin plug** Right **Room phone**

🔟 Accommodation Tips

1 Book Online
Where possible, consider booking upmarket hotels online. At many places you'll get a cheaper rate. Portugal Hotel Guide has an online booking link, as does the Portugal Travel Guide.

2 Haggle Over Room Rates
Room rates plummet out of season but it's still worth haggling over a price to determine the bottom line. This is especially so if you're a family or a small group. After all, no hotel likes empty beds. You may also be able to conjure up a deal if you decide you want to stay longer than originally planned. Try and negotiate a "package" if the hotel isn't expecting to fill up.

3 Share the Room with Your Children
Children under the age of eight are entitled to 50 per cent discount in many hotels and guesthouses if they share their parents' room. Enquire about this possibility before checking in. It's also a good idea to see the room before accepting it.

4 Time Your Golfing Holiday
Remember that if considering a golfing holiday in the Algarve, the main season is from November to March and early April. The region's golf courses get very busy in December and again in late January, February and March. The hotels linked with golf courses offer their guests preferential green fee rates, which can save the dedicated golfer a considerable amount.

5 Seek Out Disabled Facilities
Accessible Portugal is a Lisbon-based travel agency specializing in wheelchair vacations and holidays for people with limited mobility. They organize tours and city breaks to various regions including the Algarve, plus other activities. Specially adapted accommodation can be sourced, and disability equipment hired.

6 Look into Long-Term Packages
Throughout the low season it's possible to rent accommodation on a long-term basis – anything up to six months. Apartments in villa complexes are a good option, as they tend to be bereft of life outside the summer season. The swimming pool may not be full, but the atmosphere will be peaceful. The best line of enquiry is through the tourism office nearest to your desired location.

7 Bring an Adapter
Electricity is 220V, 50Hz, and plugs normally have two round pins. So bring an adapter for shavers, hairdryers etc.

8 Pack an Insect Repellent
Rooms in rural hotels invariably attract annoying flying bugs, especially mosquitoes. It's a good idea to pack a slow-burning insect repellent coil and let it smoke for an hour or so before retiring to bed.

9 Avoid Using the Room Phone
Direct-dial hotel telephone charges in Portugal are extortionate compared to those in the rest of Europe. Avoid them unless absolutely necessary.

10 Use the Hotel Fax & Internet
In contrast to phoning from your room, fax and Internet prices from *pensões* and *residenciais* are often considerably lower than using the post office where the rates are unreasonably high.

Directory

Online Booking
www.hotelguide.pt
www.portugaltravel
guide.com

Discounted Rail Fares
(808) 208 208
• www.cp.pt

Accessible Portugal
Rua João Freitas
Branco 21D, Lisbon
• (217) 203 130 • www.
accessibleportugal.com

Left **Sheraton Algarve** Centre **Le Meridien Penina** Right **Vila Vita Parc**

🔟 Luxury, Five-Star Hotels

1 Hotel Quinta do Lago

Overlooking Ria Formosa lagoon and the ocean, this sophisticated resort has two great restaurants, the Brisa do Mar (traditional Portuguese cuisine) and Cá d'Oro (famed for its Italian gastronomy). Leisure facilities include golf and a health club with gym, sauna and massage. 🅂 Quinta do Lago, near Almancil • Map J5 • (289) 350 350 • www.hotelquinta dolago.com • €€€€€

2 Vila Vita Parc

An exclusive clifftop estate set in lush sub-tropical gardens reflecting Moorish-style architecture. Accommodation is in the main hotel or in sumptuous villa suites. There's golf, in- and outdoor pools, tennis courts and a natural therapy centre. The Ocean Restaurant has two Michelin stars. 🅂 Alporchinhos, Porches, Armação de Pêra • Map F5 • (282) 310 100 • www. vilavitaparc.com • €€€€€

3 Le Meridien Penina Golf & Resort

Surrounded by verdant woodland, the Penina has an 18-hole championship golf course (see p46) and a further two 9-hole courses. Four restaurants, a beach club, watersports and a health centre complete the package. 🅂 8501-952 Portimão • Map E4 • (282) 420 200 • www.lemeridienpenina. com • €€€€

4 Blue & Green Vilalara Thalassa

Vilalara features one of the world's finest thalassotherapy (sea-water bathing) centres and an extensive range of facilities and treatments for health, beauty and wellbeing. Two excellent restaurants are also on hand. 🅂 Praia das Gaivotas, Porches, Lagoa • Map F5 • (282) 320 000 • www. vilalararesort.com • €€€€€

5 Hotel Martinhal

A blend of contemporary design and natural simplicity distinguishes this family-friendly property. All rooms offer glorious ocean views. The O Terraço restaurant (see p67) features a kids' play area. 🅂 Martinhal Beach Resort & Hotel, Quinta do Martinhal, Sagres • Map B6 • (282) 620 026 • www. martinhal.com • €€€€

6 Sheraton Algarve Hotel & Resort

Perched above some of the Algarve's best beaches, features include a childrens' entertainment village, a spa and a 9-hole golf course. All rooms have sun terraces, and guests have access to a private beach club. 🅂 Praia da Falésia, Albufeira • Map G5 • (289) 500 100 • www. sheratonalgarve.com • €€€€€

7 Vila Joya Boutique Resort

An exclusive gourmet retreat, with splendid seafront gardens and a two-star Michelin restaurant. Spa facilities and Ayurvedic massage. 🅂 Praia de Galé, Albufeira • Map G5 • (289) 591 795 • www.vilajoya.com • €€€€€

8 Tivoli Marina Vilamoura

Set right on the beach, so every bedroom balcony has stunning views of either the sea or the marina. A range of water sports are close at hand, and the Chilli Restaurant, with its panoramic vista, is ideal for formal dining. 🅂 Vilamoura marina • Map H5 • (289) 303 303 • www. tivolihotels.com • €€€€€

9 Longevity Wellness Resort

Facilities at this hotel include the Longevity Medical Spa, with its emphasis on preventive medicine. Traditional beauty treatments are also offered. The Olivier restaurant serves healthy gourmet cuisine. 🅂 Lugar do Montinho, Monchique • Map E3 • (282) 240 110 • www.longevitywellness resort.com • €€€

10 Hilton Vilamoura as Cascatas Golf Resort & Spa

The hotel's facilities include six swimming pools, cascading waterways, a luxury spa, excellent restaurant and Paradise Island kids club. 🅂 Rua da Torre d'Agua, Vilamoura • Map H5 • (289) 304 000 • www.hilton vilamouraresort.com • €€€€

Note: Unless otherwise stated, all hotels accept credit cards, have en-suite bathrooms and air conditioning

Price Categories

For a standard,
double room per
night (with breakfast
if included), taxes
and extra charges.

€	under €50
€€	€50–€100
€€€	€100–€200
€€€€	€200–€300
€€€€€	over €300

Left **Tivoli Lagos** Right **Tivoli Carvoeiro**

🔟 Four-Star Hotels

1 Vila Monte
This upscale property is located inland but is only a 15 minutes' drive from the beach. The villa-style accommodation is of singular design and character. Guest amenities include the gourmet Orangerie restaurant, the boutique Kasbah Spa, and a 3-hole pitch-and-putt golf course and driving-range. ⚲ Sítio dos Caliços, Moncarapacho • Map L5 • (289) 790 790 • www.vilamonte.com • €€€

2 Tivoli Carvoeiro
Commanding views over precipitous cliffs, this hotel is within easy walking distance of Carvoeiro town centre. The interior is Moorish in influence and rooms have spectacular ocean vistas. The health club has a Jacuzzi, sauna and Turkish bath, and there is a diving school near the bay. ⚲ Vale do Covo, Carvoeiro • Map E5 • (282) 351 100 • www.tivolihotels.com • €€€

3 Hotel Vila Galé Albacora
Converted from former fishermen's houses, the hotel promotes ecotourism and has a diving centre (see p12). Most rooms have views of Ria Formosa. Courtesy boat transport is offered to nearby Tavira island. ⚲ Apartado 2, Quatro Aguas, Tavira • Map M4 • (281) 380 800 • Closed Nov–Feb • www.vilagale.pt • €€€€

4 Estalagem Abrigo da Montanha
This granite, mountain inn is set in terraced gardens bursting with a fine collection of camellias. The views are spectacular, especially from the side of the pool. ⚲ Corte Pereira Estrada da Fóia, Monchique • Map E3 • (282) 912 131 • www.abrigoda montanha.com • €€

5 Pousada Palácio de Estói
The ancestral home of the Viscount of Estói has been carefully renovated. A contemporary wing was attached to create a luxurious pousada with ceiling murals, a spa, swimming pool and French gardens. ⚲ Palácio de Estói, Estói • Map K5 • (289) 990 150 • www.pousadas.pt • €€€€

6 Memmo Baleeira
Memmo's stylish rooms enjoy picturesque garden and harbour views. Facilities include an excellent restaurant, spa, gym and pool. There's also a surf centre where outdoor activities can be booked. Reservations recommended for August. ⚲ Sítio da Baleeira, Sagres • Map B6 • (282) 624 212 • www.memmohotels.com • €€€

7 Guadiana River Hotel
Unrivalled as the best hotel along the Guadiana, guests here wake up to a view of the river and rural Spain beyond. An ideal place to relax. ⚲ Estalagem do Guadiana, Alcoutim • Map P1 • (281) 540 120 • www.grupofbarata.com/pt • €€€

8 Tivoli Lagos
Near the old town, this smart hotel is a series of buildings linked around a swimming pool. Guests also have the use of an exclusive beach club down on the seafront. ⚲ Rua António Crisógono Dos Santos, Lagos • Map D5 • (282) 790 079 • www.tivolihotels.com • €€€

9 Hotel Eva
Very comfortable and conveniently situated right on Faro's marina, the panorama from the rooftop swimming pool is outstanding and takes in the Ria Formosa and the surrounding lagoons. The city's historic old quarter is a five-minute walk away. ⚲ Avda da República, 1, Faro • Map K6 • (289) 001 000 • www.tdhotels.com • €€€

10 Albergaria Vila Lido
Jacqueline Kennedy was a guest here in the days when this immaculately kept inn was a private villa. Light floods the verandah in late afternoon, and tea on the terrace comes with a fabulous sea view. ⚲ Avenida Tômas Cabreira, Praia da Rocha • Map E5 • (282) 424 127 • Closed mid-Nov–mid-Mar • www.hotelvilalido.com • €€

Left **Hotel Termal** Right **Hotel Colina dos Mouras**

Three-Star Hotels

1 Hotel Globo
A striking colour scheme greets visitors at this smart hotel in Portimão's historic centre. There is a superb panoramic restaurant and the leisure facilities include a sauna and Turkish bath. Close to Praia da Rocha and Autódromo Internacional do Algarve (see p72). ◊ *Rua 5 de Outubro 26, Portimão • Map E4 • (282) 405 030 • www. hoteisalgarvesol.pt • €€*

2 Alcazar Hotel
Clean, comfortable beachfront accommodation ideal for couples. The Alxazar Hotel has won plaudits for its excellent customer service and hearty breakfasts. There's a bar and two outdoor pools. An ideal base for exploring the eastern Algarve. ◊ *Rua de Ceuta 9, Monte Gordo • Map P4 • (281) 510 140 • www.hotel alcazaralgarve.com • €€€*

3 Alte Hotel
Alte is one of the prettiest villages in the Algarve, surrounded as it is by the Serra do Caldeirão mountains. The views from the hotel are stunning although its position at the summit of a hill means that having your own transport is useful. Leisure activities include a swimming pool, tennis court and billiards. ◊ *Estrada de Sta. Margarida, Montinho-Alte • Map H3 • (289) 478 523 • www. altehotel.com • €€*

4 Hotel Colina dos Mouros
A cracking view of Silves castle is to be had from this friendly hotel, just a few minutes' walk from the historic quarter. A sun terrace overlooks a circular pool and rows of orange groves. ◊ *Pocinho Santo, Silves • Map F4 • (282) 440 420 • www. colinahotels.com • €€*

5 Loulé Jardim
Refurbished to an early 20th-century design, the beige-and-cream façade faces a quiet park in the centre of Loulé. The town's castle and Saturday market are both within easy reach, and the rooftop pool is a bonus. ◊ *Praça Manuel de Arriaga, 8100 Loulé • Map J4 • (289) 413 094/5 • www.loulejar dimhotel.com • €€*

6 Hotel Termal
The Monchique Spa is set within this secluded hotel. Guests can book a range of treatments including mud bath and wine therapy. ◊ *Villa Termal das Caldas de Monchique Spa Resort, Caldas de Monchique • Map E3 • (282) 910 910 • www. monchiquetermas.com • €€€*

7 Hotel Califórnia
Within Albufeira's lively bar district, this is the ideal place if heady nightlife is your bag. All bedrooms have terrace views over the town, and Praia dos Pescadores is a 10-minute stroll away,

though the rooftop pool is just as blissful. ◊ *Rua Cândido dos Reis, 12, Albufeira • Map G5 • (289) 583 400 • Breakfast not included • www.california hotelalbufeira.com • €€*

8 Hotel Residencial Salema
The hotel building is the centrepiece of an old quay that retains the charm of colourful boats and rows of fishermen's huts. The rooms have great views of the bay, and a number of bars, cafés and restaurants are all within easy reach. ◊ *Rua 28 de Janeiro, Salema • Map C5 • (282) 695 328 • www. hotelsalema.com • €€*

9 Hotel Riomar
This hotel is in the heart of Lagos, and each room has a balcony overlooking the city. The major historical attractions are less than a 10-minute walk away, as are the shops and some great restaurants. ◊ *Rua Cândido dos Reis, 83, Lagos • Map D5 • (282) 770 130 • www. hotelriomarlagos.com • €€*

10 Hotel Dom Bernardo
The front rooms of this tidy hotel overlook the Ermida Nossa Senhora da Esperança; top floors command city centre views. Convenient for Faro's main attractions. ◊ *Rua General Teófilo da Trindade, 20, Faro • Map K6 • (289) 889 800 • www. bestwestern.com • €€*

Note: Unless otherwise stated, all hotels accept credit cards, have en-suite bathrooms and air conditioning

Price Categories

For a standard, double room per night (with breakfast if included), taxes and extra charges.

€	under €50
€€	€50–€100
€€€	€100–€200
€€€€	€200–€300
€€€€€	over €300

Left **Residencial Pensão Limas** Centre **Residencial Ponte Romana** Right **Matos Pereira**

🔟 Pensões and Residencias

1 Residencial Ponte Romana
Standing by the Roman bridge on the south side of the River Arade, this location is hard to beat. The riverside rooms face the castle, and the evening view alone is worth the stay. The restaurant serves generous portions of delicious country food. ✆ *Ponte Romana, Silves • Map F4 • (282) 443 275 • Breakfast not included • €*

2 Residencial Mira-douro da Serra
The hotel name means "mountain viewpoint" and the panorama from this hilltop hideaway doesn't disappoint. Excellent value and a great base for hill walking or pottering about the pleasant market town. All rooms have balcony views. ✆ *Rua Combatentes do Ultramar, Monchique • Map E3 • (282) 912 163 • No credit cards • No air conditioning • €*

3 Pensão Boémia
From its backstreet location, the light and airy Boémia exudes bonhomie. The top-floor rooms have balconies with views across the town's maze of white-washed homes. Breakfast not included. ✆ *Rua da Cerca, 20, Olhão • Map L5 • (962) 569 388 • No credit cards • €€*

4 Residencial Pensão Limas
Wedged between bars and restaurants in a narrow, pedestrianized street, Limas' bright yellow sun blinds grace a whitewashed façade. The staircase inside is steep and narrow, and leads to modest bedrooms. ✆ *Rua da Liberdade, 25–27, Albufeira • Map G5 • (289) 514 025 • No credit cards • €*

5 Casa Azul
Stylish, bright and colourful, this superior guesthouse has captured the imagination of surfers and city slickers alike. Its central position makes it ideal for Sagres' buzzing nightlife. Advance booking recommended. ✆ *Rua Patrão António Faustino, Sagres • Map B6 • (282) 624 856 • No credit cards • €€€*

6 Residencial Lagôas
Polished black and white azulejos decorate the façade of this well-known pensão. Its proximity to the historic centre of Tavira makes it very popular in summer, so phone ahead to check room availability. ✆ *Rua Almirante Cândido dos Reis, 24, Tavira • Map M4 • (281) 328 243 • No credit cards • No air conditioning • €*

7 Pensão Residencial Oceano
A mere stone's throw from Faro's historical quarter, this pensão in the shape of a traditional town house is also handy for shops, restaurants, cafés and the local tourism office. ✆ *Travessa Ivens, 21, Faro • Map K6 • (289) 823 349 • Air conditioning in some rooms • €€*

8 Pensão Luar
Some of the rooms here overlook the sweeping River Seixe valley, and this friendly pensão is ideal for the beach at Odeceixe. While secluded, this area is popular in summer so booking is advisable. ✆ *Rua da Vázea, 28, Odeceixe • Map C1 • (282) 947 194 • No credit cards • No air conditioning • €€*

9 Residência Matos Pereira
Set in a pedestrianized street, the Residência looks like a typical town house, matched by an atmosphere that is both domestic and jovial. ✆ *Rua Dr Sousa Martins, 57, Vila Real de Santo António • Map P4 • (281) 543 325 • No credit cards • Air conditioning in some rooms • €*

10 Casa Beny
A spruce property, located in the centre of Loulé. The smart, well-appointed rooms all have a TV and fridge, and guests also have access to a very handy rooftop terrace, where superb views of the castle can be enjoyed. Rates do not include breakfast. ✆ *Rua São Domingos, 13, Loulé • Map J4 • (289) 417 702 • No credit cards • No air conditioning • €*

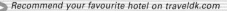

Left **Le Meridien Penina** Centre **Hotel Quinta do Lago** Right **Vila Vita Parc**

TOP 10 Hotels with Golf Courses

1 Le Meridien Penina Golf & Resort

Guests of this five-star resort have the privileged use of the 18-hole Sir Henry Cotton layout *(see p46)*, which has hosted the Portuguese Open several times. There are two 9-hole courses too *(see p48)*. ✆ *Penina 8501-952 Portimão • Map E4 • (282) 420 200 • www.lemeridien penina.com • €€€€*

2 Sheraton Algarve Hotel & Resort

The 18th hole of the hotel's spectacular clifftop course is known as the "Devil's Parlour": a long shot from the tee must carry over a deep chasm in order to reach the final green. The course and luxury hotel form the hub of the exclusive Pine Cliffs resort. ✆ *Praia da Falésia, Albufeira • Map G5 • (289) 500 100 • www.sheraton algarve.com • €€€€€*

3 Hotel Quinta do Lago

The hotel is within one of the most luxurious golfing resorts in Europe. It encompasses no fewer than three championship courses, including the par 72 Quinta do Lago South. Six more layouts are within easy reach. The hotel offers special golf tuition packages and there are special green fee rates for guests. ✆ *Quinta do Lago, Almancil • Map J5 • (289) 350 350 • www.quintadolagohotel. com • €€€€€*

4 Dona Filipa & San Lorenzo Golf Resort

This resort offers five-star accommodation, and priority of play at the par 72 scenic masterpiece is given to hotel guests. ✆ *Vale do Lobo, Almancil • Map J5 • (289) 357 200 • www.donafilipahotel.com • €€€€€*

5 Pestana Alvor Praia

An ideal five-star base for golfers, with generous discounts offered at a dozen nearby courses, including Pestana's Pinta and Gramacho layouts at Carvoeiro, home of the David Leadbetter Golf Academy. The hotel overlooks Três Irmãos beach and is close to the fishing village of Alvor. ✆ *Praia dos Três Irmãos, Alvor • Map D5 • (282) 400 900 • www.pestana.com • €€€€*

6 Tivoli Marina Vilamoura

A luxurious five-star hotel near the beach and marina, offering special golf packages. A free shuttle service operates to the Vilamoura courses Pinhal, Laguna, Millennium, Vila Sol and Old Course. ✆ *Vilamoura marina • Map H5 • (289) 303 303 • www. tivolihotels.com • €€€€€*

7 Pestana Vila Sol Golf & Spa Resort

A renowned 18-hole Championship golf course designed by architect Donald Steel, meanders around this five-star resort via several exciting water features. ✆ *Morgadinhos, near Vilamoura • Map J5 • (289) 320 320 • www. pestana.com • €€€*

8 Dom Pedro Golf Resort

This plush, modern hotel is a favourite with Algarve golfers. Facilities include a golf department where useful golf clinics can be arranged. Guests can also take advantage of privileged green fee rates at a selection of the region's top courses. ✆ *Rua Atlântico, Vilamoura • Map H5 • (289) 300 780 • www.dompedro.com • €€€€€*

9 Vila Vita Parc

A luxury resort with its own 9-hole course within the grounds, as well as a driving range and practice green. Tuition can also be arranged, with access to 20 of the Algarve's best courses. ✆ *Alporchinhos, Porches, Armação de Pêra • Map F5 • (282) 310 100 • www.vila vitaparc.com • €€€€€*

10 Tivoli Victoria

Most rooms overlook the sweeping Oceânico golf course *(see p47)* designed by Arnold Palmer. The venue has hosted the PGA Portugal Masters several times. ✆ *Avenida dos Descobrimentos, Vilamoura • Map H5 • (289) 317 000 • www. tivolihotels.com • €€€€*

Note: Unless otherwise stated, all hotels accept credit cards, have en-suite bathrooms and air conditioning

Price Categories

For a standard, double room per night (with breakfast if included), taxes and extra charges.

€	under €50
€€	€50–€100
€€€	€100–€200
€€€€	€200–€300
€€€€€	over €300

Left **Belavista da Luz** Right **Dom Pedro Marina**

🔟 Resort Hotels for Families

1 Martinhal Beach Resort & Hotel

Ideal for families with children of all ages, this resort offers spacious and stylishly designed accommodation. The restaurants and spa are also family friendly. The fashionable hotel section is more suited to couples. ◈ *Quinta do Martinhal, near Sagres • Map B6 • (282) 240 200 • www. martinhal.com • €€€€*

2 Pestana Alvor Park

Attractive aparthotel and villa complex. Its facilities include indoor and outdoor pools, a sauna, gym and games room. A children's fun centre is complemented by nearby golf, tennis and watersports facilities. ◈ *Quinta do Ribeiro, Alvor • Map D5 • (282) 000 500 • Babysitting available • www.pestana.com • €€€*

3 Hotel Algarve Casino

The complete family holiday package. As well as the famous beach, leisure facilities on hand include a swimming pool, video room, a children's zone and a casino that stages cabaret. ◈ *Avenida Tomás Cabreira, Praia da Rocha • Map E5 • (282) 402 000 • www.algarve casinohotel.com • €€€*

4 Hotel Casabela

Views across the mouth of the River Arade and close proximity to the pretty fishing village of Ferragudo form a big part of Casabela's appeal. Two swimming pools, one specially adapted for children, a tennis court and pleasant gardens complete the draw. ◈ *Vale da Areia, Ferragudo • Map E5 • (282) 490 650 • www. hotel-casabela.com • €€€€*

5 Hotel Belavista da Luz

A family-run hotel, built in a horseshoe shape to enclose two inviting pools and a "children's zone". Golf, horse riding, walking tours and scuba diving can be organized by staff. ◈ *Praia da Luz, Lagos • Map C5 • (282) 788 655 • Babysitting available with advance notice • www. belavistadaluz.com • €€€*

6 Vila Galé Albacora

A buzzing children's club and packed schedule of entertainments keep guests fully occupied. Two swimming pools, a diving centre and nearby beaches at Ilha de Tavira make it ideal for families. ◈ *Quatro Águas, Tavira • Map M4 • (281) 380 800 • www.vilagale.pt • €€€*

7 Holiday Inn Algarve

Enjoying a prime position on one of the Algarve's most popular beaches, the facilities here include an outdoor pool, games room and hair salon. The Raj Restaurant offers choice Indian cuisine. ◈ *Avenida Beira Mar, Apartado 1, Armação de Pêra • Map F5 • (282) 320 260 • Babysitting available • www.hialgarve.com • €€€*

8 Blue & Green The Lake Spa Resort

One of the pools here is designed as a shallow lake with a sandy beach. Spacious apartments are available, and there is a spa and three restaurants. Youngsters have use of the Koala Club, with activities. ◈ *Praia da Falésia, Vilamoura • Map H5 • (289) 320 700 • Babysitting available with advance notice • www.thelakeresort. com • €€€*

9 Hotel Dom Pedro Marina

With its own exclusive beach next to Vilamoura marina, this is a popular choice. Facilities include outdoor pools and a restaurant specializing in fine Italian cuisine. ◈ *Rua Tivoli, Vilamoura • Map H5 • (289) 300 780 • Babysitting available • www.dompedro.com • €€€*

10 Grande Real Santa Eulália Resort & Hotel Spa

This five-star resort has direct beach access and offers pampering at its Real Spa Thalasso. Children can try juggling and other activities at the complimentary kids' club. ◈ *Praia de Santa Eulália, Albufeira • Map G5 • (289) 598 000 • Babysitting with advance notice • www. granderealsantaeulalia resorthotelspa.com • €€€*

Left **Pousada de Tavira** Centre **Quinta do Caracol** Right **Fazenda Nova Country House**

Unusual Places to Stay

1 Pousada de Tavira – Convento da Graça

The original convent was founded in 1569 by King Sebastião and is situated near to the town's castle. Today, the old convent's mix of Baroque and Renaissance architecture makes it a stunning setting for a modern *pousada*. The 16th-century cloisters are worth a visit in themselves. ◉ *Rua D. Paio Peres Correira, Tavira • Map M4 • (281) 329 040 • www.pousadas.pt • €€€€*

2 Quinta Das Achadas

This refurbished family-run farmhouse is set in wonderful gardens on a tranquil, 3-hectare site. There's a swimming pool, an outdoor jacuzzi and a children's play area. Dinner can be provided on request. ◉ *Estrada da Barragem, 8600-251 Odiaxère • Map D4 • (282) 798 425 • No air conditioning • www.algarveholiday. net • €€€*

3 Fazenda Nova Country House

This British-run Portuguese country house has ten large suites, nine with a private garden or terrace, and self-contained apartments. Traditional architecture is mixed with fresh and contemporary interior design. ◉ *Estiramentens, Santo Estevão • Map M4 • (911) 113 039 • www.fazenda nova.eu • €€€*

4 Quinta do Caracol

A 17th-century farm lovingly converted into a series of beautiful apartments named after flowers. Birdsong from the garden aviary drifts over the shaded, outdoor dining areas. ◉ *Rua São Pedro, Tavira • Map M4 • (281) 322 475 • www. quintadocaracol.com • €€€*

5 Bela Vista Hotel & Spa

The architecture of this former *palacete* has been retained, but the look is contemporary. Guests can savour modern Portuguese cuisine, and there is a swimming pool and spa. ◉ *Avenida Tomás Cabreira, Praia da Rocha • Map E5 • (282) 460 280 • No disabled access • www. hotelbelavista.com • €€€*

6 Albergaria Bica Boa

Wooden floors and ceilings impart a rustic feel to this mountain inn, perched on the lip of a valley, a few minutes' walk out of Monchique. Just four guest rooms and fine vegetarian food. ◉ *Estrada de Lisboa, Monchique • Map E3 • (282) 912 271 • No air conditioning • €*

7 Vila Valverde Design & Country House

An upscale boutique hotel with 15 individually decorated rooms. Amenities include heated indoor and outdoor pools plus a fitness centre. ◉ *Estrada da Praia da Luz, Valverde • Map C5 • (282) 790 790 • No disabled access • www.vilavalverde. com • €€€*

8 Aldeia da Pedralva

An entire country village has been carefully restored to offer self-catering stays in wonderfully authentic whitewashed cottages. With a shop and bar-restaurant, Pedralva is charm re-invented. ◉ *Pedralva, north of Vila do Bispo • Map B4 • (282) 639 342 • No air conditioning • www. aldeiadapedralva.com • €€€*

9 Casa da Palmeirinha

This Portuguese town house with terracotta floors and *azulejos* panels has a Mediterranean feel. A flourishing roof garden looks over a central patio and modest swimming pool. ◉ *Rua da Igreja, 1, Mexilhoeira Grande, Portimão • Map D4 • (282) 969 277 • No credit cards • No air conditioning • www. solaresdeportugal.pt • €€*

10 Forte de São João da Barra

This 17th-century fort overlooks the crystal blue lagoons of the Ria Formosa. The lovely spruce gardens incorporate a swimming pool. Breakfast is served in the Governor's house. ◉ *Barroca, Cabanas • Map N4 • (281) 370 495 • www.fortesadesao joaodabarra.com • No air conditioning • €€€*

Note: Unless otherwise stated, all hotels accept credit cards, have en-suite bathrooms and air conditioning

Price Categories

For a standard, double room per night (with breakfast if included), taxes and extra charges.

€	under €50
€€	€50–€100
€€€	€100–€200
€€€€	€200–€300
€€€€€	over €300

Left **Albufeira Camping** Right **Parque de Campismo São Miguel**

Campsites

1 Quinta dos Carriços

Set in a pretty valley, this site offers all necessary facilities – toilets, hot showers, laundry rooms, shops and restaurant. There are studios and apartments for rent, and a private area for naturists. ✪ *Parque de Campismo, Quinta dos Carriços, Praia da Salema, Budens • Map C5 • (282) 695 201 • www.quintados carricos.com • €*

2 Camping Olhão

This excellent site near the Parque Natural da Ria Formosa has first-class amenities and lively recreation facilities that include a swimming pool and tennis court. There's also a mini-market, a restaurant and a bar. ✪ *Pinheiros de Marim, Apartado 300, Olhão • Map L5 • (289) 700 300 • www.algarve-gids.com • €*

3 Albufeira Camping

A sprawling camping and caravan site about 2 km (1 mile) from town, with three pools, an adventure playground, an à la carte restaurant, a supermarket and a night club. ✪ *Estrada de Ferreiras, Albufeira • Map G5 • (289) 587 629 • www. campingalbufeira.net • €*

4 Parque de Campismo São Miguel

Secluded under a canopy of pine, this is one of the most modern sites in southern Portugal. Facilities include tennis courts, pool and restaurant, and the surrounding countryside is national park. Caravans and bungalows can be hired. ✪ *São Miguel, near Odeceixe • Map C1 • (282) 947 145 • www.camping saomiguel.com • €*

5 Parque de Campismo Ilha de Tavira

Only tents go up on this island, which is car- and caravan-free. There are supermarket and restaurant facilities, and tent hire is possible too. Get there via ferry at Quatro Águas. The site's hugely popular in summer, so call ahead and ask about special promotions. ✪ *Ilha de Tavira • Map M5 • (281) 321 709 • Open mid-Apr–end Sep • No credit cards • www. campingtavira.com • €*

6 Parque de Campismo Sagres

It's not uncommon to see surfboards outside the tents and cabins here as the site's in easy reach of some fine surfing beaches. Amenities are excellent, and Sagres town is 2 km (1 mile) away. ✪ *Cerro das Moitas, Sagres • Map B6 • (282) 624 371 • www.orbitur.pt • €*

7 Parque de Campismo de Armação de Pêra

The nearest campsite to Armação de Pêra, this is great for budget travellers craving the sights and nightlife of a lively resort. Modern facilities abound on site, and it's also possible to hire bungalows here. ✪ *8365-184 Armação de Pêra • Map F5 • (282) 312 260 • www.camping-armacao-pera.com • €*

8 Parque de Campismo de Monte Gordo

The conifer woodland near the site is home to the largest population of Mediterranean chameleon in Portugal. Walks here are superb, and Monte Gordo itself is a thriving little town with an ideal beach for sunbathing and swimming. ✪ *Monte Gordo • Map P4 • (281) 510 970 • www.algarve-gids.com • €*

9 Parque de Campismo Serrão

Conveniently located near some of the western Algarve's best beaches. The facilities include a swimming pool and bungalows to rent, two with wheelchair access. ✪ *Herdade do Serrão, Aljezur • Map C3 • (282) 990 220 • www. campingserrao.com • €*

10 Camping Valverde

This site has 600 plots for tents, which can be hired on-site if needed. There are also bungalows and apartments. Book ahead in summer. ✪ *Estrada da Praia da Luz, Valverde • Map C5 • (282) 789 211 • www.orbitur.com/ campsite-orbitur-valverde • €*

Left **Hostel sign** Centre **Alcoutim youth hostel** Right **Pousada da Juventude Portimão**

TOP 10 Hostels

1 Pousada da Juventude Lagos

Slap bang in one of the Algarve's best-known resorts, this youth hostel is popular year-round. Airy rooms and dorms surround a courtyard studded with dwarf palms. ✆ *Rua Lançarote de Freitas, 50, Lagos • Map D5 • (282) 761 970 • No air conditioning • www.pousadasjuventude.pt • €*

2 Pousada de Juventude Arrifana – Aljezur

A modern and friendly hostel, not far from Aljezur, popular with surfers and those looking to get away from the crowds. A cluster of lively bars overlook the nearby beach. ✆ *Urbanização Arrifana, Praia da Arrifana • (282) 997 455 • www.pousadasjuventude.pt • €*

3 Pousada da Juventude Alcoutim

This out-of-the-way hostel overlooks River Guadiana, where it's possible to go on canoeing expeditions. There's also a swimming pool, bike rental, table tennis and snooker. ✆ *Alcoutim • Map P1 • (281) 546 004 • www.pousadasjuventude.pt • €*

4 Pousada da Juventude Faro

Handily sited if you want advice on jobs and youth discounts from the Instituto Português da Juventude. Also close to Faro's historic centre and ferries to the Ria Formosa sand dune islands. ✆ *Rua da Policia de Segurança, Pública 1, Edifício do IPJ, Faro • Map K6 • (289) 878 090 • No air conditioning • www.pousadasjuventude.pt • €*

5 Pousada da Juventude Portimão

Situated about 4 km (2 miles) north of town, the hostel – which is spacious and inviting – makes up for its lack of proximity to the beach and sights with a tennis court and pool. There is also an indoor billiards and table tennis area. ✆ *Rua da Nossa Senhora da Conceição, Portimão • Map E4 • (282) 491 804 • No air conditioning • www.pousadasjuventude.pt • €*

6 Pousada da Juventude Tavira

Ideally placed for Tavira's wealth of historical attractions and the beaches and islets of the Ria Formosa. Clean, comfortable and modern, this friendly 62-room hostel gets extremely busy in summer so advance booking is advised. ✆ *Rua Miguel Bombarda 36–38 • Map M4 • (281) 326 731 • www.pousadasjuventude.pt • €*

7 Amazigh Hostel

Independent hostel Amazigh offers budget accommodation with a dash of retro style. Double and multiple rooms are available, with public areas featuring Wi-Fi and plasma TV. ✆ *Rua da Ladeira 5, Alezur • Map C3 • (282) 997 502 • No air conditioning • Breakfast not included • www.amazighostel.com • €*

8 Pousada da Juventude Beja (Alentejo)

A modern facility within 20 minutes' walk of Beja's cultural attractions. Free Internet access available, as well as a games room and laundry. ✆ *Rua Prof. Janeiro Acabado, 7800 Beja • (284) 325 458 • No air conditioning • www.pousadasjuventude.pt • €*

9 Lagos Escape Hostel

This is ideal for budget travellers seeking a young vibe. Rooms include doubles and private and mixed dorms with shared bathrooms. Guests can use the nearby health club and restaurant. ✆ *Rua Gil Vicente 26, Lagos • (282) 767 347 • No air conditioning • No credit cards • www.lagos-escape-hostel.com • €*

10 Pousada da Juventude Almograve (Alentejo)

Enjoying an enviable coastal location, this hostel offers Internet access on site and some great beaches close by. Apartments are also available. ✆ *Rua do Chafariz, Almograve, near Odemira • (283) 640 000 • No air conditioning • www.pousadasjuventude.pt • €*

Price Categories

For a standard, double room per night (with breakfast if included), taxes and extra charges.

€	under €50
€€	€50–€100
€€€	€100–€200
€€€€	€200–€300
€€€€€	over €300

Left **Villa interior** Right **Holiday villa with roof terrace**

TOP 10 Self-Catering Agents

1 Travel Algarve
A UK agency that specializes in providing holiday breaks in villas and selected hotels in the Algarve. The number of bedrooms in the villas varies from one to six. Special offers are available from time to time. ◎ *10 Edge View, Merrymans Lane, Alderley Edge, Cheshire, UK • (0156) 588 9134 • www.travelalgarve.com*

2 Algarve Retreats
A holiday company that lists a variety of carefully selected quality villas, apartments and hotels in the western Algarve and the historic town of Lagos. The specialist agency can also arrange car hire on your behalf. ◎ *Algarve Retreats Ltd, 8 Gypsum Way, Draycott in the Clay, Ashbourne, Derbyshire, UK • (0128) 382 1072 • www.algarve-retreats.com*

3 The Villa Agency
With plenty of properties along the coastline from Almancil to Burgau (most with swimming pools), this agency's website is well designed and easy to navigate. For each property there is a comprehensive description as well as interior and exterior photographs. ◎ *31 Meeting House Lane, The Lanes, Brighton BN1 1HB, UK • (0127) 374 7811 • www.thevillaagency.co.uk*

4 Truly Algarve
This comprehensive site specialises in private villa and apartment rentals with extensive accommodation and availability in all the major resorts. It is also worth checking the "Villa of the Week" page. ◎ *Regus House 1, The Friary, Temple Quay, Bristol BS1 6EA, UK • (0845) 003 8272 • www.villa-in-algarve.co.uk*

5 Algarve Rentals
Simple to use, this attractive website lists a wide variety of properties to rent throughout the region, both in lively resorts and in more secluded areas. The home page also features a selection of last-minute rentals. ◎ *20 Barnton Street, Stirling, Stirlingshire FK8 1NE, UK • (0141) 416 2967 • www.algarve-rentals.com*

6 Villa Plus
An extensive catalogue of luxury villas with private swimming pools for rent located in some of the most sought-after areas in the Algarve. The website is well illustrated throughout with colour photographs of the villas. ◎ *Drover House, 16 Adelaide Street, St Albans, Hertfordshire, UK • (0172) 783 6686 • www.villaplus.com*

7 The Real Algarve
A handpicked portfolio of the finest holiday villas, resort property, town houses and farmhouses for rent or sale. ◎ *Tamarind, Brackenhill, Caythorpe, Nottinghamshire, UK • (0115) 966 3661 • www.therealalgarve.com*

8 Villas International
A first-class website that is clear, precise and well illustrated. The Algarve region is covered well, and properties are regularly inspected and updated. Local representation is usually provided and car hire can be arranged. ◎ *17 Fox Lane, San Anselmo, CA, USA • (415) 499 9490 or (800) 221 2260 • www.villasintl.com*

9 Great Rentals
Great Rentals lists a variety of luxury villas from across the Algarve. Each entry is illustrated with images of the property, along with specifications and contact details. ◎ *3801 S. Capital of Texas Hwy, Suite 150, Austin, Texas, USA • (512) 493 0368 • www.greatrentals.com*

10 Homeaway
The entire region is covered here, particularly Lagos, Carvoeiro, Albufeira and the Loulé area. Property descriptions are detailed, and prices listed are per week. Reviews are also given. ◎ *1011 W. 5th Street, Suite 300, Austin, Texas, USA • (877) 228 3145 • www.homeaway.com*

Index

Acknowledgements

The Author

Paul Bernhardt is a freelance travel writer, blogger and photographer who lives in Portugal.

Produced by BLUE ISLAND PUBLISHING

Editorial Director Rosalyn Thiro
Art Director Stephen Bere
Associate Editor Michael Ellis
Designer Lee Redmond
Picture Research Ellen Root
Research Assistance Amaia Allende
Main Photographers
Paul Bernhardt, Linda Whitwam
Additional Photography Paul Bernhardt, Rough Guides/Eddie Gerald, Rough Guides/Matthew Hancock
Index Jane Simmonds
Fact Checker Mark Harding, Paul Bernhardt

AT DORLING KINDERSLEY
Publisher Douglas Amrine
Managing Editor Anna Streiffert
Senior Art Editors Marisa Renzullo, Ian Midson
Senior Cartographic Editor
Casper Morris
DTP Jason Little
Production Melanie Dowland
Revisions Team Marta Bescos Sanchez, Nadia Bonomally, Juliet Kenny, Maite Lantaron, Carly Madden, Hayley Maher, Nicola Malone, Alison McGill, Catherine Palmi, Helen Partington, Pollyanna Poulter, Amir Reuveni, Simon Ryder, Collette Sadler, Sands Publishing Solutions, Conrad van Dyk, Dora Whitaker

Picture Credits

The publishers would like to thank all the museums, archaeological sites, hotels, restaurants, bars, clubs, shops, galleries and other establishments for their assistance and kind permission to photograph at their establishments.

Placement Key: a=above; b=below; c=centre; f=far; l=left; r=right; t=top

ARTE ALGARVE: 16br; ASSOCIAÇÂO TURISMO DO ALGARVE: CM LOULÉ – MIRA: 58tr. PAUL BERNHARDT: 58tl, 59t, 66c, 67tl, 81tl. CÂMARA MUNICIPAL DE LOULÉ: Helga Serodio 19clb. MARY EVANS PICTURE LIBRARY: 34tr, 34b, 35tr. FAZ GOSTOS: 89tc; FAZENDA NOVA: 128tr. GETTY IMAGES/HULTON ARCHIVE: Keystone 35tl. HOTEL TERMAL: 124tl. LAGOS SELECT: 66tr; LAGOS SURF CENTER: 98tl; LÁGRIMAS HOTELS & EMOTIONS: 89ca; LEONARDO MEDIA LTD: 123tl. MARTINHAL BEACH RESORT & HOTEL: 99tl; MOVIJOVEM: 130tr; MUSEU ARQUEOLOGICO, ALBUFEIRA: 44tl; MUSEU DR.JOSE FORMOSINHO DE LAGOS: 22tl, 22tr, 22c, 23tl; MUSEU MARITIMO, FARO: Carlos Porfirio 45b. NOSOLOÁGUA: 62tl. QUINTA DAS ACHADAS: 131tc; QUINTA DO FRANCÊS VINEYARD: 15cla. REGAIAO TURISMO DO ALGARVE: 58tc; ROBERTHARDING.COM: 44bl, 44br, 45t. TRAVEL LIBRARY: Stuart Black 1, 94–5. VILA VITA PARC/STROMBERGER PR: 66tc. PETER WILSON: 12–13.

All other images are © Dorling Kindersley. For further information see www.dkimages.com.Pull Out Map intro panel both images DK IMAGES: Rough Guides/Eddie Gerald.

Cartography Credits

James Macdonald, Rob Clynes (Mapping Ideas Ltd).

Phrase Book

In an Emergency

Help!	**Socorro!**	soo-**koh**-roo
Stop!	**Páre!**	pahr'
Call a doctor!	**Chame um médico!**	shahm' ooñ meh-dee-koo
Call an ambulance!	**Chame uma ambulância!**	shahm' oo-muh añ-boo-lañ-see-uh
Call the police!	**Chame a polícia!**	shahm' uh poo-**lee**-see-uh
Call the fire brigade!	**Chame os bombeiros!**	shahm' oosh bom-**bay**-roosh
Where is the nearest telephone?	**Há um telefone aqui perto?**	ah ooñ te-le-**fon'** uh-**kee** pehr-too
Where is the nearest hospital?	**Onde é o hospital mais próximo?**	ond' **eh** oo ohsh-pee-tahl' mysh pro-see-moo

Communication Essentials

Yes	**Sim**	seeñ
No	**Não**	nowñ
Please	**Por favor/ Faz favor**	poor fuh-**vor** fash fuh-**vor**
Thank you	**Obrigado/da**	o-bree-**gah**-doo/duh
Excuse me	**Desculpe**	dish-**koolp'**
Hello	**Olá**	oh-**lah**
Goodbye	**Adeus**	a-**deh**-oosh
Good morning	**Bom-dia**	boñ **dee**-uh
Good afternoon	**Boa-tarde**	boh-uh tard'
Good night	**Boa-noite**	boh-uh noyt'
Yesterday	**Ontem**	oñ-tayñ
Today	**Hoje**	ohj'
Tomorrow	**Amanhã**	ah-mañ yañ
Here	**Aqui**	uh-**kee**
There	**Ali**	uh-**lee**
What?	**O quê?**	oo keh
Which?	**Qual?**	kwahl'
When?	**Quando?**	kwañ-doo
Why?	**Porquê?**	poor-keh
Where?	**Onde?**	oñd'

Useful Phrases

How are you?	**Como está?**	koh-moo shtah
Very well, thank you.	**Bem, obrigado/da.**	bayñ o-bree-gah-doo/duh
Pleased to meet you.	**Encantado/da.**	eñ-kañ-**tah**-doo/duh
See you soon.	**Alté logo.**	uh-**teh** loh-goo
That's fine.	**Está bem.**	shtah bayñ
Where is/are...?	**Onde está/ estão...?**	ond' shtah/ shtowñ
How far is it to...?	**A que distância fica...?**	uh kee dish-**tañ**-see-uh **fee**-kuh
Which way to...?	**Como se vai para...?**	koh-moo seh vy puh-ruh
Do you speak English?	**Fala Inglês?**	**fah**-luh eeñ-glehsh
I don't understand.	**Não compreendo.**	nowñ kom-pree-**eñ**-doo
I'm sorry.	**Desculpe.**	dish-**koolp'**
Could you speak more slowly please?	**Pode falar mais devagar por favor?**	pohd' fuh-lar mysh d'-va-**gar** poor fah-**vor**

Useful Words

big	**grande**	grañd'
small	**pequeno**	pe-**keh**-noo
hot	**quente**	keñt'
cold	**frio**	free-oo
good	**bom**	boñ
bad	**mau**	**mah**-oo
enough	**bastante**	bash-**tañt'**
well	**bem**	bayñ
open	**aberto**	a-**behr**-too
closed	**fechado**	fe-**shah**-doo
left	**esquerda**	shkehr-duh
right	**direita**	dee-**ray**-tuh
straight on	**em frente**	ayñ freñt'
near	**perto**	**pehr**-too
far	**longe**	loñj'
up	**suba**	**soo**-bah
down	**desça**	**deh**-shuh
early	**cedo**	**seh**-doo
late	**tarde**	tard'
entrance	**entrada**	eñ-**trah**-duh
exit	**saída**	sa-**ee**-duh
toilets	**casa de banho**	**kah**-zuh d' **bañ**-yoo
more	**mais**	mysh
less	**menos**	**meh**-noosh

Making a Telephone Call

I'd like to place an international call.	**Queria fazer uma chamada internacional.**	**kree**-uh fuh-**zehr** oo-muh sha-**mah**-duh in-ter-na-**see**-oo-**nahl'**
a local call	**uma chamada local**	**oo**-muh sha-**mah**-duh loo-**kahl'**
Can I leave a message?	**Posso deixar uma mensagem?**	**poh**-soo day-shar oo-muh meñ-**sah**-jayñ

Shopping

How much does this cost?	**Quanto custa isto?**	**kwañ**-too **koosh**-tuh eesh-too
I would like...	**Queria...**	**kree**-uh
I'm just looking.	**Estou só a ver obrigado/a.**	shtoh soh uh vehr o-bree-**gah**-doo/uh
Do you take credit cards?	**Aceita cartões de crédito?**	uh-**say**-tuh kar-toinsh de **kreh**-dee-too?
What time do you open?	**A que horas abre?**	uh kee oh-rash **ah**-bre?
What time do you close?	**A que horas fecha?**	uh kee oh-rash **fay**-shuh?
this one	**este**	ehst'
that one	**esse**	ehss'
expensive	**caro**	**kah**-roo
cheap	**barato**	buh-**rah**-too
size (clothes/shoes)	**número**	**noom'**-roo
white	**branco**	**brañ**-koo
black	**preto**	**preh**-too
red	**roxo**	**roh**-shoo
yellow	**amarelo**	uh-muh-**reh**-loo
green	**verde**	**vehrd'**
blue	**azul**	uh-**zool'**

Types of Shop

antique shop	**loja de antiguidades**	**loh**-juh de añ-tee-gwee-**dahd'sh**
bakery	**padaria**	**pah**-duh-**ree**-uh
bank	**banco**	**bañ**-koo
bookshop	**livraria**	lee-vruh-**ree**-uh
butcher	**talho**	**tah**-lyoo
cake shop	**pastelaria**	pash-te-luh-**ree**-uh
chemist	**farmácia**	far-**mah**-see-uh
fishmonger	**peixaria**	pay-shuh-**ree**-uh
hair dresser	**cabeleireiro**	kab'-lay-**ray**-roo
market	**mercado**	mehr-**kah**-doo
newsagent	**kiosque**	kee-**yohsk'**
post office	**correios**	koo-**ray**-oosh
shoe shop	**sapataria**	suh-puh-tuh-**ree**-uh
supermarket	**supermercado**	soo-**pehr**-mer-**kah**-doo
tobacconist	**tabacaria**	tuh-buh-kuh-**ree**-uh
travel agency	**agência de viagens**	uh-jen-**see**-uh de vee-**ah**-jayñsh

Sightseeing

cathedral	**sé**	seh
church	**igreja**	ee-**gray**-juh
garden	**jardim**	jar-**deeñ**
library	**biblioteca**	bee-blee-oo-**teh**-kuh
museum	**museu**	**moo**-zeh-oo
tourist information	**posto de turismo**	posh-**too** d' too-**reesh**-moo
closed for holidays	**fechado para férias**	fe-**sha**-doo puh-ruh **feh**-ree-ash
bus station	**estação de autocarros**	shta-sowñ d' oh-too-**kah**-roosh
railway station	**estação de comboios**	shta-**sowñ** d' koñ-**boy**-oosh
azulejo	uh-zoo-**lay**-joo	painted ceramic tile
Manuelino	ma-noo-el-**ee**-oo	Manueline (late Gothic architectural style)

Staying in a Hotel

Do you have a vacant room?	**Tem um quarto livre?**	**tayñ** ooñ **kwar**-too **leevr'**
room with a bath	**um quarto com casa de banho**	ooñ **kwar**-too koñ **kah**-zuh d' bañ-**yoo**
shower	**duche**	**doosh**
single room	**quarto individual**	**kwar**-too een-dee-vee-doo-**ahl'**
double room	**quarto de casal**	**kwar**-too d' kuh-**zhal'**
twin room	**quarto com duas camas**	**kwar**-too koñ **doo**-ash kah-mash
porter	**porteiro**	poor-**tay**-roo
key	**chave**	**shahv'**
I have a reservation.	**Tenho um quarto reservado.**	**tayñ**-yoo ooñ **kwar**-too re-ser-**vah**-doo

Eating Out

Have you got a table for …?	**Tem uma mesa para … ?**	**tayñ** oo-muh **meh**-zuh puh-ruh
I'd like to reserve a table.	**Quero reservar una mesa.**	**keh**-roo re-zehr-**var** oo-muh **meh**-zuh
The bill, please.	**A conta por favor/faz favor.**	uh **kohn**-tuh poor fuh-**vor/fash** fuh-**vor**
I am a vegetarian.	**Sou vegetariano/a.**	Soh ve-je-tuh-ree-**ah**-noo/uh
Waiter!	**Por favor!/Faz favor!**	poor fuh-**vor** fash fuh-**vor**
the menu	**a lista**	uh **leesh**-tuh
fixed-price menu	**a ementa turística**	uh ee-**mehñ**-tuh too-**reesh**-tee-kuh
wine list	**a lista de vinhos**	uh **leesh**-tuh de **veeñ**-yoosh
glass	**um copo**	ooñ **koh**-poo
bottle	**uma garrafa**	oo-muh guh-**rah**-fuh
half bottle	**meia-garrafa**	**may**-uh guh-**rah**-fuh
knife	**uma faca**	oo-mah **fah**-kuh
fork	**um garfo**	ooñ **gar**-foo
spoon	**uma colher**	oo-muh kool-**yair**
plate	**um prato**	ooñ **prah**-too
breakfast	**pequeno-almoço**	pe-**keh**-noo-ahl-**moh**-soo
lunch	**almoço**	ahl-**moh**-soo
dinner	**jantar**	jan-**tar**
cover	**couvert**	koo-**vehr**
starter	**entrada**	eñ-**trah**-duh
main course	**prato principal**	**prah**-too prin-see-**pahl'**
dish of the day	**prato do dia**	**prah**-too doo **dee**-uh
set dish	**combinado**	koñ-bee-**nah**-doo
half portion	**meia-dose**	may-uh **doh**-se
dessert	**sobremesa**	**soh**-bre-**meh**-zuh
rare	**mal passado**	**mahl'** puh-**sah**-doo
medium	**médio**	**meh**-dee-oo
well done	**bem passado**	**bayñ** puh-**sah**-doo

Menu Decoder

abacate	uh-buh-**kaht'**	avocado
açorda	uh-**sor**-duh	bread-based stew (often seafood)
açúcar	uh-soo-**kar**	sugar
água mineral	**ah**-gwuh mee-ne-**rahl'**	mineral water
alho	**ay**-oo	garlic
alperce	ahl'-**pehrce**	apricot
amêijoas	uh-may-**joo**-ash	clams
ananás	uh-nuh-**nahsh**	pineapple
arroz	uh-**rohsh**	rice
assado	uh-**sah**-doo	baked
atum	uh-**tooñ**	tuna
aves	**ah**-vesh	poultry
azeite	uh-**zayt'**	olive oil
azeitonas	uh-zay-**toh**-nash	olives
bacalhau	buh-kuh-**lyow**	dried, salted cod

143

banana	buh-**nah**-nuh	banana
batatas	buh-**tah**-tash	potatoes
batatas fritas	buh-**tah**-tash **free**-tash	french fries
batido	buh-**tee**-doo	milk-shake
bica	**bee**-kuh	espresso
bife	**beef**	steak
bolacha	boo-**lah**-shuh	biscuit
bolo	**boh**-loo	cake
borrego	boo-**reh**-goo	lamb
caça	**kah**-ssuh	game
café	kuh-**feh**	coffee
camarões	kuh-muh-**roysh**	large prawns
caracóis	kuh-ruh-**koysh**	snails
caranguejo	kuh-rañ **gay**-yoo	crabs
carne	**karn'**	meat
cataplana	kuh-tuh-**plah**-nah	sealed wok used to steam dishes
cebola	se-**boh**-luh	onion
cerveja	sehr-**vay**-juh	beer
chá	**shah**	tea
cherne	**shern'**	stone bass
chocolate	shoh-koh-**laht'**	chocolate
chocos	**shoh**-koosh	cuttlefish
chouriço	shoh-**ree**-soo	red, spicy sausage
churrasco	shoo-**rash**-coo	on the spit
cogumelos	koo-goo-**meh**-loosh	mushrooms
cozido	koo-**zee**-doo	boiled
enguias	eñ-**gee**-ash	eels
fiambre	fee-**añbr'**	ham
fígado	**fee**-guh-doo	liver
frango	**frañ**-goo	chicken
frito	**free**-too	fried
fruta	**froo**-tuh	fruit
gambas	**gañ**-bash	prawns
gelado	je-**lah**-doo	ice cream
gelo	**jeh**-loo	ice
goraz	goo-**rash**	bream
grelhado	grel-**yah**-doo	grilled
iscas	**eesh**-kash	marinated liver
lagosta	luh-**gohsh**-tuh	lobster
laranja	luh **rañ**-juh	orange
leite	**layt'**	milk
limão	lee-**mowñ**	lemon
limonada	lee-moo-**nah**-duh	lemonade
linguado	leeñ-**gwah**-doo	sole
lulas	**loo**-lash	squid
maçã	muh-**sañ**	apple
manteiga	mañ-**tay**-guh	butter
mariscos	muh-**reesh**-koosh	seafood
meia-de-leite	**may**-uh-d' **layt'**	white coffee
ostras	**osh**-trash	oysters
ovos	**oh**-voosh	eggs
pão	**powñ**	bread
pastel	pash-**tehl'**	cake
pato	**pah**-too	duck
peixe	**paysh'**	fish
peixe-espada	**paysh'**-shpah-duh	scabbard fish
pimenta	pee-**meñ**-tuh	pepper
polvo	**pohl'**-voo	octopus
porco	**por**-coo	pork
queijo	**kay**-joo	cheese
sal	**sahl'**	salt
salada	suh-**lah**-duh	salad
salsichas	sahl-**see**-shash	sausages
sandes	**sañ**-desh	sandwich
sopa	**soh**-puh	soup
sumo	**soo**-moo	juice
tamboril	tañ-boo-**ril'**	monkfish
tarte	**tart'**	pie/cake

tomate	too-**maht'**	tomato
torrada	too-**rah**-duh	toast
tosta	**tohsh**-tuh	toasted sandwich
vinagre	vee-**nah**-gre	vinegar
vinho branco	veeñ-yoo **brañ**-koo	white wine
vinho tinto	veeñ-yoo **teeñ**-too	red wine
vitela	vee-**teh**-luh	veal

Numbers

0	zero	**zeh**-roo
1	um	**ooñ**
2	dois	**doysh**
3	três	**tresh**
4	quatro	**kwa**-troo
5	cinco	**seeñ**-koo
6	seis	**saysh**
7	sete	**set'**
8	oito	**oy**-too
9	nove	**nov'**
10	dez	**desh**
11	onze	**oñz'**
12	doze	**doz'**
13	treze	**trez'**
14	catorze	ka-**torz'**
15	quinze	**keeñz'**
16	dezasseis	de-zuh-**saysh**
17	dezassete	de-zuh-**set'**
18	dezoito	de-**zoy**-too
19	dezanove	de-zuh-**nov'**
20	vinte	**veent'**
21	vinte e um	**veen**-tee-ooñ
30	trinta	**treeñ**-tuh
40	quarenta	kwa-**reñ**-tuh
50	cinquenta	seen-**kweñ**-tuh
60	sessenta	se-**señ**-tuh
70	setenta	se-**teñ**-tuh
80	oitenta	oy-**teñ**-tuh
90	noventa	noo-**veñ**-tuh
100	cem	**sayñ**
101	cento e um	**señ**-too-ee-ooñ
102	cento e dois	**señ**-too-ee-doysh
200	duzentos	doo-**zeñ**-toosh
300	trezentos	tre-**zeñ**-toosh
400	quatrocentos	**kwa**-troo-**señ**-toosh
500	quinhentos	kee-**nyeñ**-toosh
600	seiscentos	saysh-**señ**-toosh
700	setecentos	set'-**señ**-toosh
800	oitocentos	**oy**-too-**señ**-toosh
900	novecentos	nov'-**señ**-toosh
1,000	mil	**meel'**

Time

one minute	um minuto	ooñ mee-**noo**-too
one hour	uma hora	**oo**-muh **oh**-ruh
half an hour	meia-hora	**may**-uh **oh**-ruh
Monday	segunda-feira	se-**goon**-duh-**fay**-ruh
Tuesday	terça-feira	ter-sa-**fay**-ruh
Wednesday	quarta-feira	**kwar**-ta-**fay**-ruh
Thursday	quinta-feira	**keen**-ta-**fay**-ruh
Friday	sexta-feira	**say**-shta-**fay**-ruh
Saturday	sábado	**sah**-ba-too
Sunday	domingo	doo-**meen**-goo